Take Back Your Future!

Take Back Your Future!

*Get Unstuck and Create the Life you
Want, Love, and Deserve*

James E. Trapp

ISBN: 978-1-64826-780-2
Printed in the United States of America

To Muhammed Ali, and my father, James Edward Trapp, Sr. Ali, who modeled what it means to follow your convictions and not be concerned with other people's opinions. My Dad, who died way too soon, but reminded those who knew him what it means to live a life of simple significance.

"It's never too late to become what you might have been."
George Elliot

CONTENTS

"You are not here to fit into society, you are here to stretch the society in which you live and make it better through the deliverance of your good."

James E. Trapp

Preface

The Secret of *The Secret*…

In 2006, *The Secret*, a personal development film based on the spiritual Law of Attraction, became an international sensation. Its popularity continues to attract new followers to this day.

The primary message of the film is that you "attract" what you want. Anything you want or desire can be attained by holding fast to the belief that it will show up if you continuously think about it while in a positive emotional state.

It is a powerful spiritual law. Celebrities such as Will Smith, Jim Carrey, and UFC champion Conor McGregor use and avow to the effectiveness of the Law of Attraction and related tools such as visualization.

However, many folks, particularly those who claim to have tried its methods and got little or no results, have severely criticized the movie and its claims. Still, others attacked *The Secret* because of its emphasis on attaining money and material goods. The critics lambasted the movie because it seemed to advocate that the universe is our personal "on-demand catalogue" that is purely there to satisfy selfish, egoic needs.

Although The Secret and its underlying principle, the Law of Attraction, represent a valid spiritual law, it is incomplete. It neither addresses the fact that material things alone cannot bring happiness nor helps us understand what genuine success is.

Moreover, *The Secret* does not identify the inner work we must do to change our self-image to not only attract what we want, but to assure we keep it once we get it.

While putting the Law of Attraction to work is essential to manifestation, it is only the beginning. There is also the unstated Law of Action—something the secular business world has mastered but often at the expense of our well-being. This book seeks to integrate and balance the two approaches.

We are here for a purpose that goes beyond securing things and making money—not that there is anything wrong with that. The material things are here for us to enjoy. However, we are also here for a purpose that's bigger than our egoic needs and goes beyond the time we are here on the planet.

Every year, a conference called Wisdom 2.0 is held in San Francisco, California. The tag line describes the essence of the conference as "*Where mindfulness meets technology.*" The conference seeks to meet one of the major challenges of our day of connecting humanity through the rapidly evolving technology while at the same time supporting our well-being and what is useful to the world.

The well-being is addressed by applying spiritual principles such as mindfulness, integrating it with technology, and secular techniques so we create a future that reflects the better angels of our nature.

This book will give you tools to use alongside the Law of Attraction that will help you create the life you want, love, and deserve. It will help you uncover the power within you so you can free yourself from the bondage that is stopping you from expressing who you have come here to be.

By applying the principles covered in this text, you can liberate your life, and express the greatness that is within you.

The steps that are covered in this book will help you answer these questions:

- W_h_a_t_ _i_s_ _g_e_n_u_i_n_e_ _s_u_c_c_e_s_s_?
- What blocks me from seeing the field of possibilities for my life? And what must I do to eliminate those blockages?
- What is the critical step I must take before I even consider what the vision is for my life or project?
- How I do I know when I am living my true vision as opposed to what just sounds good?
- What are the tools for the journey I need to use in order to ensure I create?
- How can I maintain the energy to do what I need to do to ensure my purpose in life manifests itself? And finally,
- Why should I think about the legacy I will leave behind?

This book will explore these topics to help you claim and exercise your power to create the life you want, love, and deserve.

In doing so, you put your future back in your hands.

Enjoy.

Chapter 1

A New Way to Define Your Success

No six-year-old child should have to endure the terrifying experience I did. But I did.

It was just another routine day until I got home from school and my mother wasn't there. A flash of intuitive angst and dread hit me. The feeling didn't last long, but I sensed that this was not good. I did not see her for the rest of the evening, and she wasn't there when I finally went to bed. Neither was she there the next morning when I woke up and got ready for school. My angst intensified, and I didn't get a satisfactory answer to what happened from my father or aunt.

Days, then weeks went by. A discomforting new norm set in once I realized my mother was not coming back. I didn't know what happened to her, where she was, or why she left. The experience left a void within me that I was neither fully conscious of nor aware of how much it would influence the trajectory of my life experience.

It seemed as if my future had been hijacked.

I sought to fill that void I thought I had within me by channeling my energy into performing exceptionally well in school. It didn't fill that perceived void, but it did pay off. Despite the financial challenges we faced, the impoverished neighborhood we lived in, I ended up being accepted to Princeton University.

I thought that such an achievement would fill the void and give me the satisfaction I longed to have. It did not. What I discovered is when we get temporary joy or fulfillment from anything outside of us, what inevitably follows is dissatisfaction. I got snagged into a collective belief system that has convinced a large swath of society that achievement and material success alone can bring us lasting happiness.

It can't.

Not realizing this truth, I sought to capture satisfaction by other means. After briefly working for the Miami Herald business division, I went to law school. Although I loved the law, one reason I became a lawyer was I believed it would fill that nagging emptiness within me. I achieved, at least by society's standards, success by practicing law for several years. Yet, the satisfaction I sought did not come. Not knowing how to get that fulfillment, I engaged in riotous living that included drug and alcohol abuse. I ended up losing everything I thought to be important and was trapped in a prison of my own making.

The Revelation…

After coming face-to-face with the truth of my being, I stumbled across seven principles and practices that liberated me from those shackles so I could create my best life here and now.

When I put those seven principles into practice, I wiped out the notion that there was something I was missing, found out what it meant to be genuinely happy, and what I have come here to be and do. I also found the tools needed to manifest my heart's desire.

To an outside observer, it would appear I was someone who rose from being in bondage to addictive substances to becoming the leader of a thriving spiritual community that helped transform thousands of lives and eventually the CEO of an international movement dedicated to positive paths for spiritual living.

What was behind the manifestation is key and can be accessed by anyone. Once accessed, you can break free from whatever is holding you back from unleashing the life you deserve.

Get Unstuck

I've been counseling and coaching people for more than 25 years. And I've discovered that an overwhelming percentage of them feel trapped in life due to bondage to something. Usually, it's a disempowering belief system of one kind or another. But these are self-created prisons and can be obliterated by waking up the inner abolitionists that can break those shackles.

A group of Harvard Business School graduates came together for their fifteenth-year reunion[1]. A decade and a half earlier, they graduated from one of the most renowned schools in the world. It seemed their destiny would be nothing but prosperity and blissful days.

---

[1] Charles Ruhig, "The Future of Work: Wealthy, Successful and Miserable, New York Times Magazine 2019"

By objective standards, that abundance and apparent euphoria became a reality based on the level of success and privilege those graduates achieved. They reached a level of achievement not seen in years. They were the financial elite. Most of them lacked nothing. But a number of them were not happy.

Why the Long Face?

Several of those successful people were outright miserable. One of the graduates ran a large hedge fund up until his investors sued him. To add insult to injury, some of the people who sued him were members of his extended family.

Another graduate had risen to a top role at a major company only to be pushed out by the vicious corporate politics within the business. One of the alumni found out a conniving partner stole her firm right from under her while she was in a maternity ward about to give birth.

These are extreme examples. But even those who were living what appeared to be ordinary lives experienced acute dissatisfaction. They compared themselves to others, talked about the promotions they did not get, and the lack of connection with their children due to spending so much time on their jobs. One graduate lamented that despite earning an annual income of over one million dollars, he endured daily stress of working with people he could not stand.

Despite the accumulation of wealth, several of the alumni believed they were wasting their lives, and there was no meaning to their existence.

Chasing Feathers in the Wind

What this scenario demonstrates is that material acquisition is not necessarily what it's cracked up to be. That's because what often follows temporary satisfaction or fulfillment from anything attained outside of ourselves or external achievement is dissatisfaction.

Jesus referred to this sense of dissatisfaction when he said to the woman at the well, "Whoever drinks the water of this well shall thirst again."[2] To put it another way, you can never get enough of something you do not need.

Seeking satisfaction through mere acquisition of things is like chasing a feather in the wind. The more one swats after it, the more it eludes you.

___

[2] 1 John 4:13

Not knowing this, in my own life, I sought to get satisfaction by chasing another feather. After briefly working for the Miami Herald, I went to law school. While I enjoyed studying law, as I previously noted, I became a lawyer as a means to fill the seemingly insatiable void that was within me. By becoming a lawyer, I achieved, at least by society's standards, success.

Yet, the satisfaction I sought did not come. Not knowing how to get that fulfillment, I engaged in riotous living, which included drug abuse that led to addiction, and I ended up losing everything that I thought was important – my career, my relationship, money, and societal status.

Another Approach to Success

How do we measure genuine success? It certainly is not solely based on how much you make or how many material possessions you acquire. On the one hand, there are real needs or the things that are essential to comfortably sustain our lives. On the other hand, there are "unnecessary necessities" we believe we must have to be successful.

If you work fifteen-hour days doing something you hate in order to chase those "unnecessary necessities," there is a point of diminishing returns. It doesn't matter how many digits you have on your paycheck, those material things can't turn a job that sucks away your soul into a good job.

In the United States, less than half of the objectively successful professionals are satisfied with their work. The remainder is neutral toward their work at best, and downright unhappy at worst. This group includes lofty professions such as medicine, law, and corporate executives.

Some of it is due to the intense competition from a global market, oppressive hours, and brutal office politics. Many of these seemingly successful but unhappy workers do not believe their work has a sense of purpose or something that goes beyond meeting their desires.

Why do you do what you do?

Contrast those Harvard Business School graduates with the late comedian Bernie Mack. By all measures, Bernie was a success by society's standards of fame, fortune, and status. During an interview, an audience member asked Bernie if he believed he would have reached his present level of achievement. And Bernie Mack said no because he didn't care and never compared himself to other people. His ultimate goal was to be his best self regardless of what showed up as a material success. He believed if he successfully fulfilled his purpose of making people laugh and met his basic needs, he would consider himself a success.

Similarly, Dave Chapelle, one of my favorite comedians, was speaking with his father about skipping college to pursue a career in show business. His dad said that acting was a lonely business, and he might not make it. Dave responded by saying that it depends on what you mean by "make it." Dave Chapelle went on to explain that if he did what he loved and made the salary of a schoolteacher, which his dad was at the time, he would consider his life a success.

The New Definition of Success

In contrast to the mentioned Harvard Business School graduates whose definition of success was based more on material acquisition, both Bernie Mack and Dave Chappelle had a different definition of success. Their characterization related to pursuing an idea that resonated with their core being. Not the pursuit of strict materiality.

To be of service to an idea is the new definition of success. When we are of service to an idea that is right and perfect for us, what comes along with that idea is abundance, unbounded energy, divine wisdom, vitality, and being a finely tuned instrument of the Universe so that you bring your unique gifts and talents to the party called life.

Whether a person considers themselves successful and feels a deep satisfaction for what they do is determined by whether they have a purpose in life. In other words, they know "why" they do what they do.

Many people simply go through the motions repeating pretty much what they have done the day before, unconscious of why they are doing what they are doing. They live to make it through the day to earn a living, and then at the end of their life, they leave the human shell without ever knowing why in the heck they came here in the first place.

Living with a purpose is the deepest part of the river of life. But many of us don't jump in the deep end of the pool of life because we go through task-oriented living only and have no goals. Others may have goals, but they have no purpose or a more substantial reason for doing what they are doing.

Satisfaction comes from living with purpose in which tasks and goals are tools to help us achieve an underlying meaning. It's about being who we have come here to be.

In the end, all we must be is ourselves. After all, no one can 'do you' better than you. To create a life that reflects authentic success, we should think about purpose and model our lives after the people who have discovered their reason for being here on the planet. Such individuals have identified their unique gifts and shared them with the world in big or small ways.

Dr. Martin Luther King, Jr. had a vision of humanity honoring the value of each other and working together for the common good.

Nelson Mandela's purpose was to build a new South Africa based on forgiveness and reconciliation. Because he had a compelling objective, he was able to endure 27 years in a South African prison as preparation to become President of the very country that imprisoned him.

People throughout history have discovered the fire in their soul and reflected their authentic selves.

But this is not about them; it's about you.

You have a unique gift and purpose you are here to uncover and share with the world as well as the people around you. Aim to share those unique gifts to benefit others. It is something that comes to you readily and naturally. It is part of your DNA and something you would happily do even if he did not get paid for it.

When you are living your purpose, time flies, and there's nothing else you'd prefer to do. When you are expressing your reason for being here on the planet, you reflect who you were born to be.

When you are living your purpose, it not only affects the people that are here but also with future generations. Your mission is inseparable from who you are; it is your gift to the world.

It is not a matter of being grandiose or being self-important. It's about making your life significant.

A prominent celebrity and businessman made his transition. One of his business acquaintances was on his way to the cemetery for the burial service. As he was driving, he noticed there was another service taking place at the same time.

There was a long line of cars heading toward the second service. Probably ten times as many people were heading there. The businessman said to himself, "The man at the service that I am attending was important in the community and very well known. But the person at this other service must have been extraordinarily important for so many people to be attending."

The businessman stopped a young man who was going toward the other service and said, "That person honored at that burial service must have done some important things in the community for so many people to show up."

The young man hesitated before responding, but eventually told the businessman, "I guess she was important. Her name was Mrs. Maggie. She was a loving and caring person. For fifty years, she was the crossing guard for all the children at the local elementary school. So all the children, their parents, and grandparents who Mrs. Maggie served all those years have come to pay their respects and appreciate the important role she played in their lives."

Mrs. Maggie may have had a simple life, but it was a life of purpose that left an indelible imprint to all those who crossed her path.

How to Uncover Your Purpose

Some people know their purpose. It becomes clear to them very early in life. However, you may be saying to yourself, "I don't know my purpose or why I am here."

In a moment, I will take you through an exercise that will help you identify your purpose. But first, let's talk about the types of gifts you have.

True Gifts vs. Near Gifts

We have true gifts, and we have near gifts. However, our ultimate goal is to express our true gifts. Let's distinguish between one's true gift and one's near gift. Your true gift is your calling and what you can uniquely do. You can have more than one true gift. Those gifts, no matter what they may be, are the reason you have taken this incarnation. You are here to release them to benefit the planet.

Then there are near gifts. Near gifts reflect things you do okay. However, they are neither your innate genius nor what you have come to the planet to do. They are gifts, nevertheless, and you may use your near gifts to help you survive or stay afloat until you can use your true gifts.

For example, you may have the gift of being a waiter or waitress when you want to act or be a spoken word artist or singer. In the meantime, you do your best as a waiter or waitress. That's good.

While you are waiting tables, you find your calling is to fellowship with people, so when you are waiter or greeter at a theatre, you heal by delivering that particular service. Somebody else may not want to be there. There are times you express your true gift and purpose by using your near gift.

How to Uncover your Purpose and True Gifts
As noted, some people know their purpose almost immediately in life. Others claim they have no idea what they have come here to do or what their gifts are. If you are in the first category, excellent! You just have to hone your skills and talents in that area, put all your energy, resources available to you so you can be the best you can be.

Others don't know what their purpose is and have no clue how to determine what it might be.

The following exercise can help you identify what your purpose is.

On a sheet paper:

1. List 6 people you admire

2. Next to the names write the traits you admire in them
3. Look for common characteristics and circle them
4. Write the top 6 attributes on a card
5. At the top of the paper, write "This is who I have come here to be"
6. At the bottom of the sheet, write, "I know they are in me because I see it in others."
7. Keep the card, to remind you if you are on your card or not and who have come here to be

Machiavelli noted that prudent person should always follow in the footsteps of great people and imitate those who have been outstanding.[3]

One of the people I identified as someone I admired is Muhammed Ali. While he was arguably the greatest heavyweight boxing champion of all time, what struck me about him was his authenticity.

Ali gave up millions of dollars and the prime years of his career when he took a stand to refuse to be drafted into the military service due to his opposition to the Vietnam War. The trait I chose to associate Ali with is "principled."

____

[3] **Niccolò Machiavelli, <u>The Prince</u>**

The list of traits on my "Who I have come here to be" card the first time I did this exercise is:

1. Spirit-led
2. Persistent
3. Authentic
4. Unleashed
5. Principled

I know this is true because I see it in others.

The Power of One Thing

The above traits can help identify how you desire to be and how you desire to show up in the world. It gives a clue as to what your purpose is. It is helpful to start by focusing on one thing to express that purpose through.

To find the one vehicle through which you can express those traits you have identified as who you have come here to be, you can ask yourself questions such as, "What do I love to do?" "What comes easy for me?" "When did I feel the greatest joy in my life?"

Also, you have an inner guidance system, your heart, that is continually sending you messages about what you should be doing with your life. Be still, listen, and follow that guidance. That guidance will reveal to you what that one thing is.

The importance of the "one thing" is found in the wisdom of a movie character. The character is named Curly; the movie is City Slickers.

In this film, there's also a character named Mitch Robins. Mitch is played by Billy Crystal, who takes a break from his Manhattan lifestyle and sets out to find himself. He meets Curly, who is the opposite of the uptight Mitch. Curly is carefree but tough and lives a balanced life.

Curly and Mitch are riding on horseback. They're talking about life. Along the way, Curly poses this question to Mitch, "Do you know what the secret of life is?"

Mitch says, "No, what?"

Curly holds up one finger.

Mitch is confused and asks, "Your finger?"

Still holding one finger, Curly says, "One thing. Just one thing. Stick to that, and everything else means nothing".

Mitch, holds up his finger, and says, "That's great. "What is the one thing?"

Curly says, "That's something you have to figure out." That one thing will help you focus on how you express your purpose.

I came across my one thing in a way I would never have imagined.

When I was in my first year of high school, my counselor called me in the office for a meeting to help me plan my curriculum. He suggested that I drop a world history class I was taking and take a course in speech and debate. I was not in any way interested in doing public speaking, but somehow he convinced me that I should give it a try.

Reluctantly, I did.

At first, I questioned whether I had made the right choice. I wasn't very good at speaking and thought I made a mistake by taking the class. But an exciting thing happened. The more I did it and participated in debate tournaments, the more I enjoyed it and the better I got at speaking.

Eventually, my partner and I were one of the best teams in Florida. It was something that served me well as a college student, a lawyer, a CEO, and a spiritual teacher.

Speaking was the vehicle in which I carried out my purpose to make a positive difference in people's lives and inspire leaders to unleash their best selves so they can achieve their boldest goals and elevate their organizations.

Putting it all together - Ask Empowering Questions

To put all the pieces together to help you find your purpose, review who you have come here to be traits, what gives you joy, as well as what comes naturally to you. You can also observe people who are doing things in life that catch your attention and inspire you to want to do the same or something similar.

Then, go into the silence and ask, "What is the highest and best thing I can do with my life through which I can express my purpose and make a difference in people's lives and the world?"

Questions are important. The quality of the answers you get depend on the quality of the questions you ask. Albert Einstein once said, if he had to solve a problem and only had one hour, he'd spend 55 minutes formulating the right question.

As that scriptural reference says, "Keep on asking, and you will receive what you're asking. Keep on seeking, and you will find. Keep on knocking, and the door will open for you."[4]

---

[4] Mathew 7:7. New Living Translation

Take Back Your Future! Practice #1

Life doesn't come with a guidebook that tells you what success is for you. You write it as you go along. Nevertheless, there are suggestions that can help you.

1. Follow your heart and intuition so you stay true to yourself.
2. Go apart from the hustle and bustle of life. While in your solitude ask, "What is mine to do that reflects who I am and brings me joy?"
3. Don't worry about what other people think.
4. Forget about the past and think about the kind of person you desire to be.
5. **_Do_** the things that bring you joy
6. Believe in yourself

Chapter 2

Drop Your False Sense of Self

I was in a funk.

In a puff of smoke - more accurately a bunch of puffs- everything I had gotten and thought was important in life was gone.

Here I was in a drug rehabilitation center wondering, "How did I end up here?"

Suddenly I was jolted out of my self-absorption as I listened to a fellow client share her story. As I observed her and took in what she had to say, I could not help but ask myself, "How in the world did *she* end up here?" She seemed to have the world in the palm of her hand.

She was an up and coming model destined for greatness. If you looked at her and felt her energetic presence, you could understand why. She radiated an aura described as the "It" factor. You can't define it, but when you are in the presence of such a person, you know it's there. She had it in spades.

I would have bet dollars to donuts she was headed straight to international stardom.

But shockingly, she did not see herself that way. She thought she was not good enough, pretty enough, or worthy of success. It was hard for anyone to believe she saw herself in that light.

To make a long story short, she not only self-destructed with drugs and alcohol, she also ended up mutilating her face. As is the case of many self-injury victims, there was tissue damage that was so bad, even the best plastic surgeon could not restore her appearance. As a result, she was no longer able to work as a model.

A dream life suddenly and tragically came crashing down.

It was sad. For a moment, I stopped thinking about my so-called problem that led me to a personal path of self-destruction (more about that later). After all, that up and coming model had won life's lottery ticket in the physical attributes department and seemed to lack nothing. Despite that, she did not see herself as worthwhile and sabotaged what appeared to be a sure success.

You may have your own experience of self-sabotage that is not as dramatic as my friend's. Perhaps you set goals for yourself and something always seems to trip you up. It doesn't happen just one time, but it is a pattern.

As you try again, there is an uneasy feeling in your gut and you end up saying to yourself, "*You know, I want to go for what my heart is telling me to do, but I'm hesitant. I'm afraid I will just screw things up. When I look back over my life, I realize that just when I am about to make things happen, all of sudden – Bam! I miss an important meeting, I say something that blows up the project, I end up mistreating someone, or I just don't follow through. I don't know why I keep messing things up.*"

The origins of this are not just the result of immediate behavior; rather, it is the by-product of something more profound. It is the image we have of ourselves or our self-concept.

How we see ourselves has a lot to do with how our life will unfold and what your experiences will be. It is essential to know you cannot go beyond how you see yourself. No matter what you have going for yourself, if you do not see yourself as deserving, you either will not be successful, or you will be unable to sustain it if you *do* reach a level of success.

Changing your self-concept is key to liberating yourself from the conditions you don't like. Over time, how we habitually see ourselves creates a groove in our mind that serves as a default way of being, acting, and how our life will manifest. What makes this particularly insidious is you may not be aware you have accepted a view of yourself that has nothing to do with who you are and what you can be.

Sometimes an incident happens, and we interpret that event in a way that creates a false and lasting view ourselves. That view creates a barrier and self-perception that we seem to be unable to go beyond.

I ran into this barrier in my life. As I examined this phenomenon, I realized that it is not something limited to a chosen few. It's a pervasive condition in a large segment of the population. As a result, to create our best lives, we must make changing our self-concept a top priority.

I didn't fully grasp this until I went to that rehab center in that non-descript building in Little Haiti section of Miami, where both that aspiring model and I were clients. The lack of self-worth was a common thread for the other clients, as well as people I have counseled or coached later in my career.

Of course, I know first-hand based on my life. My perceived abandonment by my mother led to a self-limiting belief about what was possible in my life. Now, that was my interpretation of what happened and what I accepted as truth, and not necessarily objective facts.

My acceptance of this interpretation of events affected me profoundly and shaped my self-concept. And as noted, we cannot go beyond the image we have of ourselves regardless of how much we have going for us.

As a result of my perception of being abandoned, I felt there was and would always be something missing in me. I attempted to fill an imaginary internal void through material acquisition and outer success as commonly determined by society. I graduated at the top of my class in high school, attended Princeton University, went to law school, and worked for a Fortune 500 company.

None of that could overcome my sense of unworthiness. In turn, this image of myself determined my mindset. That mindset contributed to my attitude and real belief, which set in motion my actions and my life experiences.

I did not address the heart of the matter that led to my self-sabotaging and self-destructive life of drugs and alcohol that I believed would fill the void. I ended up destroying and losing everything I thought was important: home, relationship, career. I didn't know what to do or where to turn.

A Defining Life Moment

But then I had one of those life-defining moments. I was before a judge that I previously represented clients. I came face to face with the God of my being. Now at the time, I wasn't into that God stuff. But in that instant, it was like the universe intervened on my behalf.

A woman who I did not know at the time, but knew me—the true me—crossed my path. Not the person I was pretending to be or had manufactured in my mind. She saw me as I could be.

The woman asked me if I wanted help. Up to that point, I was in denial that I needed any help. But for some reason, I said yes.

As I look back, I've come to realize there is power when we say "yes" to the universe in those humble moments. Genuine humility means to be open and teachable. A "yes" in such circumstances can marshal forces around us to support us in ways we could not imagine.

As a result of me saying yes, I ended up at Concept House, where I began to learn the principles of what it takes to create our best lives.

Burying those false self-concepts

The first thing we must do is recognize and destroy the false self we have created. That's another one of those, "Easy for you to say" statements.

It comes down to changing our paradigms. Paradigm is a fancy way to describe how we think. Most of us habitually think, and those patterns of thought become embedded in the fabric of our being. The unconscious thoughts pose the most significant challenge. They are the ones lodged below the surface of the conscious mind.

We reinforce these thoughts by the actions we take on a day to day basis. It goes without saying that if we do the same things day in and day out, it's impossible to create a life different from the one we already have. To create a new future for ourselves and interrupt the cycle of self-sabotage, we have to take a different action.

Frequently, our life is like the movie *Groundhog Day*. We shut off the alarm like we did all the previous days. We get out of bed on the same side, slip on the same slippers, and turn on the lights as we always do. Then we likely go through the same bathroom routine as we have the last ten years, do our hair the same way (if you have hair, mine is long gone), drink the same coffee, then arrive at work via the same route. Once at work, we do the same things the same way we always have done.

Finally, when the day ends, most of us go home and prepare for the next day by rinsing and repeating what we did the day before. All the while, the thoughts and the subsequent actions remain the same.

Thoughts Matter

From time to time, we are shackled by negative self-sabotaging thoughts that lead to behavior that inevitably stops us from fulfilling our purpose. We have between 25,000 and 50,000 ruminations per day. Some of them are good positive thoughts.

Others, not so much. You may have said to yourself, "I can't do that!" "That's way too difficult for me!" "If I try, I will just screw up."

Or we may imagine some make-believe person saying, "Who do you think you are?" Such statements seem like they are coming from a brutal or cruel person with a mission to destroy our self-confidence. However, that tyrant comes from within our minds. Or, as Jesus said, "Our foes are within our household."[5]Infuse such thoughts with energy, and they lead to behavior that stops us from achieving our dreams and the fulfillment of our purpose. Often, they are on autopilot, and we are not consciously aware that our self-sabotaging behavior is the by-product of those thoughts.

Instead, we attribute our lack of success or not having what we want in life to bad luck.

Change Your State, Change Your Experience
The first thing we must do to move beyond the previous formation of our life—which transformation is—we must become conscious of the state of being we are in when making choices that do not lead to creating our best lives.

---

[5] Matthew 10:36 New Revised Standard Version

We can assess whether we are in a low state of mind by observing our physical bodies. When we feel anything in our life, we feel it through our physical bodies.

Imagine a depressed person. I then ask you to describe their physical presence. You would likely have an accurate description if you said, "He's slumped over, with his head and eyes down, and his breathing is shallow. Plus, his facial muscles are down and slack as opposed to up and tight." When anyone is in a low or depressed state, we can tell by observing their body.

Mindfulness meditation helps determine your state of mind as well. You can observe your thoughts, and when you do, you will likely be surprised at what shows up.

To rise above the behavior that does not support the creation of our best lives here and now, we must replace our routine actions that have become a habit with new habits and behaviors. We need a whole new way of thinking from which we operate. To achieve this new way of thinking, we have to decide not to make the same choices we did the day before. Decide means that we cut away anything that is not in alignment with what we want in life.

Now once we decide to think and feel differently about ourselves and take different actions, it will feel uncomfortable. We've changed how we have habitually acted, and it's disrupting our familiar and conditioned pattern of living. Then we start hearing those tyrannical voices in our head telling us, "This does not feel good," "I'm uncomfortable," or "Just do what you've always done."

It may sound something like:

> Self: "I'm going to quit my job and go
> after my dreams."
> Habitual thinking: "Sit yo' ass down!"
> Self: "Okay."

If we succumb to that inner tyrant, we will revert to our conditioned state and paradigm. This decision point is the most challenging moment to make a change because it is tough to stop acting as we have habitually done. When we reach that crucial point, we feel uncertain. The old self is dying, and the new has yet to take hold. We've stepped into a void. However, it is the perfect place to create what we want in life.

If we can become comfortable with being in that place and stay in that unknown space long enough, we can create a new future for ourselves. The future is unpredictable and a little scary. But if you want to predict the future, you have to invent it!

The best place to invent it is in the unknown space. We'll get more into how you can create a future that you align with your authentic self in the next chapter.

In the meantime, know that if you start thinking about how you will act differently, you will begin creating a whole new paradigm on how you will show up in this world. Rather than believing the circumstances make it impossible for you to achieve your goal, you start looking for the possibilities. Or instead of waiting to be grateful for a future event to take place, you will give thanks right now, even before you see the physical manifestation.

What happens when you live in this paradigm? You pull away from your past and drawn to your future self. Emotionally, when you feel that future in the present moment, you have exponentially increased the chances it will show up in and as your life. That's because emotionally, you are living in the future and not devotedly attached to your past experiences and that fervidly charged future will chase you down.

Now I will talk more about how this aspect of the creation process works in the next chapter on *Taking Back Your Future*. But let me give you one example that I stumbled upon years ago in my life.

I had recently left Concept House and moved into a pretty bare efficiency. It had the basic furnishings I needed to have to get by: a bed, dresser, chair, and refrigerator. But it was empty. So I knew I wanted to completely furnish the place and decorate it to make it comfortable and feel like home. I didn't have money to buy what I wanted. However, without being prompted or told to do so, I looked around the room. I then envisioned in my mind everything I wanted to have in the place.

What I saw in my imagination was the sofa I wanted, the desk and chair that would be ideal for me to use as a study, the lamp that would be on the writing-table, the rugs, the drapes over the windows, and even the pictures on the walls. I saw everything in a flash in detail.

Then I forgot about it. Fast forward two months later, as I was asking around if anyone had any furniture they wanted to get rid of on the cheap, I ended up speaking to the manager of a store in the design district in Miami, Florida, where I worked. He mentioned that his sister had passed away and left him a bunch of furniture that he had no need for, and asked if I had use for any of it. I said, "Let me see. I'll check it out."

When I saw the furniture, I was shocked. The furnishings matched what I had seen when I envisioned that efficiency wholly furnished. Now I probably shouldn't have been surprised, but I was. It gave me an idea of what can happen when I release the past and open myself up to a new future.

That manifestation was a small event in the scheme of things, but it was huge as far as demonstrating the power of picturing myself in a future that did not yet exist.

The idea is to release attachment to a way of thinking that does not serve us so a new way of thinking can emerge.

So how do we release that old way of thinking and create a new paradigm we are not only emotionally connected to but also pulls us to a future we want?

It is useful to first get clear on what we mean by paradigm. A paradigm is a mental program that has dominant control of our habitual behavior. Most of our action is habitual. Although we think we are in control, more often than not, paradigms are controlling our lives.

Time for A Shift

Twin brothers had the same opportunities and upbringing and excellent education. Yet one put his knowledge to work to be very successful, and the other brother seemed to fail at everything he did. What was the difference? They developed different paradigms—one was that of success and belief in himself, and the other was one of struggle and lack of self-worth. So even if the twin who met a string of failures in life worked twice as hard, he would not get different results because his paradigm or way of thinking stayed the same from one year to the next.

When paradigms control our thinking and subsequent behavior, our lives will continue to be as it always has been and nothing changes.

Paradigm Shifting

So how do we shift a paradigm that does not serve us?

First, after we have identified the thoughts that no longer serve us, we must loosen the grip they have over us by practicing the technique of release. It sounds something like this, "I release the belief that I am prone to illness." Or "I release the thought that I am not worthy." Or, "I release the belief I am not good enough"—whatever the dominant thought is within your particular paradigm.

Then to further shift the paradigm, you must consistently repeat ideas that are the opposite of the pattern of thought we currently have. This repetition is spaced out over time until it becomes part of the fabric of your unconscious mind. So how could that show up? It can be along the lines of, "I am healthy and whole." "I am infinitely valuable" "I am more than good enough."

To add fuel to the power of the paradigm-shifting process, interject an emotional charge to the new ideas you are repeating to yourself. You can do so by first thinking of an event that has had an uplifting and lasting influence on you. Then associate that emotion with the repeated statement. It can be the birth of your child, the love you have for a family member or even a pet. It can be how you felt when you witnessed an unselfish act that one human being showed to another. It can also be a scene in a movie that emotionally affects you every time you think about it.

In any event, when you start stating your new ideas and think of that emotional moment, the fresh approach will stick with you on a profound level, you will displace the old belief that no longer serves you, and a new paradigm will begin to emerge.

To this day, even though he is now a young man, whenever I think about when my son was born, I get a powerful emotional charge. When I recall that event, and I affirm a new idea or vision, that idea sticks to me more intensely than if I just stated the words without that association. And that new paradigm begins to fortify itself in my life.

Feel the Emotional Uplift

Another way to up-level the emotional power of repetition of ideas is to imagine the benefits that will result when your new future happens. Maybe your family is taken care of, and you see in your mind's eye, their happy faces. Perhaps it's the ability to send deserving kids on a trip that broadens their horizon of opportunities they would not ordinarily have. This imagined future changes the direction of their lives and makes your heart sing.

Repetition with emotion means a paradigm shift and the creation of new life experiences.

It is Done Unto You as You Believe

It all starts with changing the beliefs that no longer serve us. I'm not talking about just the conscious thoughts. They are not the most important ones. No, the real power of our paradigms lies in the beliefs we are unconscious of—the ones that are mostly invisible to us. They are the ones that are running our life.

But if we don't know what these unconscious beliefs are, how can we change them? Uncovering this is easier said than done. However, you can begin by identifying such thoughts by objectively examining every aspect of your life. Such an examination will be a good indication of what you truly believe.

There is a biblical statement that says, "You shall know them by their fruits."[6] In this case, you can look at where you are right now in life and trace the experiences back to the thoughts from which they

---

[6] Mathew 7:20 New Revised Standard Version

have come. That includes our physical body and the body of affairs, also known as our life.

What you have created outside of yourself is directly correlated to what is going on within you. Take notice of what you have manifested and become aware that you have likely repeated several times over. These manifestations demonstrate the tremendous power that is within you.

Unlearn, Unlearn

To get a sneak preview of how you can unlearn old thoughts and create an opening for new ideas for a better future, here is what you can do:

Look at two choices you have made that did not advance the creation of your best life.

Next, determine what the underlying beliefs you have had that led to your less than ideal behavior or actions.

Then ask, "What are the emotions behind those thoughts and behaviors?"

Then make a new choice for your life.

Then decide the thoughts and behaviors that serve the creation of the future you want and rehearse them in your mind until they become the new paradigms for going forward in your life.

Feel Your Future – Now!

To work, put yourself in a state of mind entirely different than the one you have been in up to that point. You have to feel your future *now*.

You do not wait for that future job to show up before you feel that you have it. Don't wait for the actual healing before you experience you are already whole. Stop holding up believing you are prosperous before you feel wealthy. No longer put love on hold while anticipating the perfect relationship to manifest. Don't hold back feeling empowered before you think you're already successful.

Lady McBeth, arguably William Shakespeare's most ambitious characters in all his work, said it this way, "Thy letters have transported me beyond this ignorant present, and I feel now the future in the instant."

You have to feel these things before they appear. When you have the sensation of it before the manifestation of the event, the demonstration will show up.

Sometimes we need practices to up-level our self-image and worthiness. These exercises will help us not backslide and fall prey to an old useless paradigm that is lurking in the background. That paradigm is waiting to pounce when we are at a vulnerable moment. So here are practices you can put to work throughout your daily living.

1. **Continuously speak words of worthiness to yourself.** When we accept a paradigm of unworthiness, it is not unusual to talk to ourselves in ways that reinforce this falsehood.

When we believe such nonsense, on some level, we are sending a message to the universe that says we are not worthy. When "The Force," also known as the creative energy of the universe hears this, it mirrors back to us experiences that reflect the words we are sending out it.

For example, if we say something like, "I don't have time to take care of myself." The universe hears this and says in substance, "If you don't have time to take care of yourself, neither do I!" And we end up getting bombarded by experiences that infringe on our precious time.

Such behavior includes such things as saying yes to everything and everyone who asks us to do something. We end up overcommitting to our detriment. It also includes accepting lame excuses from ourselves as to why we are not committing to our life's vision. It also encompasses staying in harmful situations beyond what is wise, productive, and damaging to us.

To reverse the messages we are telling ourselves and the world around us, every morning before we start our day, we can speak aloud "I AM" statements. Such statements can be:

- "I am only to receive good in my life."
- "I am deserving of the best the world has to offer."
- "I am love."
- "I am doing what supports my highest self."
- "I am power."

Identify a statement you can affirm before starting your day.

Say it to yourself as you are looking in the mirror. Do this for 40 days straight. If you miss a day, start over until you reach the 40 days. You will begin to erode the old paradigm and replace it with one that reflects your real value.

Change your energetic state. In addition to speaking affirmatively to yourself, you can augment your self-value by changing your energetic state.

To change your state, you first need to be aware of your current state. Let's go back to our previous example of someone who is depressed. This time imagine you are in a sad or funky state of mind. Step back and envision an image of yourself. Then ask, "What picture of myself am I expressing?" What energy am I radiating?"

Most likely, you are a slumped over, with constricted posture and shallow breathing. You're probably a dull speaking pile of mess.

Such behavior is not the way to feel good about yourself. You can transform that low energetic state by changing your posture.

For example, when you are feeling down and less than your ideal positive self, you can simply shift your posture to a superhero power pose in which you stand erect, hands on hips, head up, as if you have just conquered the world. By standing in a confident posture, even when you don't necessarily feel confident, you will raise your energetic state that can lead to decisive action that matches that level of energy.

Increase your self-discipline. In this case, determine what the most important thing is you can do right now. Then do it. To make this work, complete a task that will lead to the realization of the stuff that is important to you.

When you complete an important milestone on something important, guess what happens? Your self-worth goes up. The regard you have for yourself increases. It can leave you exhilarated and release the natural happy drug—endorphins that are within every person. You will become motivated to do even more and with greater and greater excellence. When you do something well, you develop more competence, and when you develop greater capability, you feel more confident and exude more self-worth.

Be clear on what you stand for. When you know what you stand for, you're less likely to fall prey to doing or succumbing to actions that don't serve you or erode how you value yourself. You will say yes to those things that support you and no to those things that do not.

You will raise your standards of what you will or will not accept in your life. You will boost your self-confidence and esteem because you say no to a request, not out of fear but out of principle. An example of taking a stand for life is to say something like, "I take a stand to be happy." When you are clear that this is who you have come here to be, it's easier to know what decisions are in congruence with your stand and those that are not.

As the lyrics to Sly and the Family Stone's song, **"Stand!"** says:

Stand!
In the end, you'll still be you.
One that's done all the things you set out to do.
Stand!
There's a cross for you to bear.
Things to go through if you're going anywhere.
Stand!

Stop trying to get others to accept you. Seeking approval from others may be a big one for you as it is for many people who connect their value to getting recognition from others.

But as the great musician and music producer Quincy Jones noted, not one drop of your self-worth is dependent on the acceptance of anyone but yourself. You can say to yourself, "What other people think of me is none of my business!"

You do not want to allow other people to give you your value. When you don't let others dictate your worth, you are no longer at the mercy of other people's view of who you are. Instead, give yourself unconditional positive self-acceptance. Remember that you are the twinkle in the eye of the creator. So twinkle!

To help us move this process forward, we have to ask the universe, God, The Force, Creator, or whatever you want to call it, "What is the highest and best that is seeking to be revealed in my life? " We will explore this next in the next chapter.

Take Back Your Future! Practice #2

To Claim Your Worth:

1. Begin your day by affirming positive words about yourself.
2. Feed your body nutritious food and drink.
3. Challenge negative thoughts you have about yourself. Whenever those thoughts arise declare, ***"This is not true!"***
4. Surround yourself with people who engage in positive, loving, and encouraging conversations.
5. Don't compare yourself to other people. Only compare yourself to your previous self.
6. Celebrate whenever you have a win.
7. Practice the word "No" (with compassion of course).

Chapter 3

Take Back Your Future!

How do you create what you want and stop settling for what you think you can have?

I recall the time I was talking to a 12-year-old middle school student. She happened to model for the "FUBU" (For Us, By Us) clothing line for kids. During our talk, I casually said that it was amazing she worked for the FUBU.

She took me aback when she said, "I don't just work at FUBU. *I AM FUBU!*" Her response was at a level of emotion and intensity I didn't expect. She was letting me know that being at FUBU was not just a fun thing to do; it was something she embodied within every cell of her being. Her parents noted, even before her first modeling job, their daughter was inseparable from FUBU.

That middle school student modeled a vital quality anyone must have to create what they want in life—emotionally embody with what you want to create.

Some people know early in life what they have come here to be. The late great Michael Jackson knew what he wanted to be at an early age—a renowned entertainer. He embodied his vision when he was a youngster and identified role models he wanted to emulate - James Brown, Sammy Davis, Jr., Gene Kelley, and the Westside Story Dancers, to name a few.

Before he became an international star, Michael was a passenger in a car with his brothers when they passed by the 90,000+ seat Los Angeles Coliseum. He said with conviction and belief, "I will perform in this Coliseum before a sold-out audience." Not only did he perform there, but in sold-out venues around the world. He was a big-time creator.

Not everyone will be a Michael Jackson, nor should they necessarily want to be. We all have something within us that is uniquely ours to do and create. But how do you know what you should create? How do you know what is uniquely yours to do?

The Starting Point - Capture Your Unique Vision

First, you must capture the right and perfect idea for your life. There is an unlimited number of things we can do in life, but within that vast field of possibilities, there is something that is for you uniquely to do. Depending on what stage of life you happen to be in, it will vary.

The first step is to ask the right questions. The perfect answer is waiting to reveal itself once you ask the right question. It is an answer that will align with the vision that is uniquely yours.

A good start is to ask, "What is the universe's or God's idea for my life?"

You must contemplate that question, reflect on it, mull it around in your consciousness, and meditate on that question.

The key is not to limit yourself. If a seemingly outlandish idea pops into your awareness, don't dismiss it. You can always scale it back later. But in the beginning, push yourself beyond your comfort zone or what you think is possible.

One way to create a future that stretches that comfort zone is to rate the initial vision you have come up with as if you were going to rate it on Yelp or a similar business review site. For example, if you were going to rate a restaurant or a company's service, you would likely rate it on a five-star scale. One star means you rated it as having lousy service; five stars would indicate it has outstanding service.

You want to do the same for your envisioned life—except for one thing. You want to create an experience that rates a ten or eleven on a five-star scale.

This idea of using such a rating system comes from the company Airbnb. They asked the question if they were to rate hosts and their homes so that the guests would have such a mind-blowing experience they would want to shout it out to the world. That's the kind of life vision you want to create.

Using the Airbnb example, if you had a one-star experience, you'd knock on the door, and no one is there to answer. No one shows up, and you are so pissed off you ask for your money back.

Perhaps a three-star experience is one when you knock on the door and it takes 15 minutes before anyone shows up. Maybe a five-star encounter is when you tap on the door someone answers immediately, lets you in, and everything meets your expectations, but nothing earth-shattering.

But what would a six-star rating be on a scale of one to five? The host opens the door and greets you with "Hi, my name is James. Welcome to my house." And the host gives you a personal guided tour, a gift, offers you a great bottle of wine, and a rare specialty treat. The host brings you over to the kitchen and opens up the fridge and says, "Help yourself to anything that you like while you are here." He shows you the bathroom stocked with high-end exotic toiletries.

You might say to yourself, "This is far better than a hotel. I will use Airbnb again. It exceeds my expectations." That's a six-star rating.

What about a seven-star rating? Perhaps in addition to what you got at the six-star level, the host knows you are learning line dancing, so he books a free lesson for you with the best local line dance teacher. And the host paid for it!

To top things off, the owner/host says, "Here are the keys to my car. You can drive to the lesson or anywhere else you want to go during your stay." Just as you think it can't get any better, the host tells you there's a reservation for dinner at the best restaurant in town.

You might say, "*Whoa*! Freakin' unbelievable and beyond anything I would have expected."

Let's skip ahead and ask, "What would a ten-star experience be on a five-star scale?" Here's where you stretch your powers of imagination to greater heights. In this scenario, it's what a world-renowned pop star like Beyonce' would experience if she landed in a country she had never been to before. Her fans are beside themselves when they learn Beyonce' is going to perform there for the first time.

A ten-star Airbnb experience would be when you get off the plane, 3,000 fans are cheering your name, with a caravan of cars welcoming you to the country. When you arrive at the house, there is a press conference for you. And if that weren't enough, when you knock on the door, your favorite entertainer or actor opens the door and says, "Welcome to my home." You are beside yourself! That's probably an eleven on a five-point scale.

A ten or eleven-star rating is the type of exercise you want to go through when seeking to create the highest and best vision for your life. Take the limits off and start by bringing this question to your time of silent reflection. "What is the universe's highest and best expression of my life?" Once you get a picture of what that is, maybe it's a six or a seven on a scale of ten; stretch your imagination until you reach the ten or eleven level.

Now it may seem out of reach based on where you are right now, but if you can imagine it and anyone else has done it, then you can do it too. Imagination is powerful. As Albert Einstein noted, "Imagination is more important than knowledge."

So that's the first step. Create a vision. You must see it in your mind first.

Everything created has been created twice—first in mind, followed by the material plane.

It is also essential to see the picture in as much detail as you can fathom. The universe responds to your detailed description. If you come up with a fuzzy picture, you'll end up with blurred results. So create as clear a picture of the future as you can.

However, there is one caveat. After describing your vision, add this sentence, "I envision this or something better." That way, you leave room for

Spirit to add to the picture. After all, this all-knowing presence may have something to add that we have overlooked.

With that qualification in mind, write down your vision. Read it twice a day—once in the morning and once just before you go to bed at night. Your unconscious mind will be working on developing ideas to make your vision come true even when you're not consciously thinking about it.

You can even go high tech and create a mind movie. A mind movie is a digital vision board that has positive affirmations, inspiring images, and motivating music. For more information about mind movies, you can go online at https://www.mindmovies.com/

What are You Willing to Become?

Spirit would not give you a vision without the means to get you there. Once you have captured that vision, the next thing you must do is determine what qualities you must possess for that vision to manifest.

The vision is not outside of you; it's something that out pictures itself based on who and what you are being. In other words, it comes from within you.

There is an axiom known as the Hermetic Principle that says in part, "As within, so without." It means that what we think about and the qualities we radiate from within ourselves will show up in our world.

For you to manifest your vision, you have to elevate the qualities that support it and eliminate the traits that do not help that imagined future become a reality.

To help you get there, pose the question, "What qualities must I embody? Is it boldness? Is it an unwavering belief in myself or my cause? Do I need to develop a "can do" mindset?"

Good Riddance to what does not serve you

To evolve, Ralph Waldo Emerson noted, we must "take our bloated nothingness out of the path of the divine circuits." That bloated nothingness is the qualities and traits we have picked up along the way in life that not only do not serve us but block and hinder the vision for our life from being expressed. No one is stopping us. We are stopping ourselves. Since we created it, we can uncreate it.

Perhaps when you were a child during the summertime, you played outside. As you played, you got thirsty, and you looked for a hose to drink water out of (I know, people don't do that anymore. Nowadays, it's bottled water or bust, but play along with me). But lo and behold, when you turn on the faucet, no water comes out. You realize you're standing on the hose. You have to take your foot off the water hose for the water to flow freely.

In the same way, you have to release those qualities that are blocking you from experiencing the full expression of your vision. Releasing requires self-awareness and to objectively inventory ourselves.

To move this along, we ask, "What qualities am I holding on to that are inhibiting me from unleashing my vision? Do I believe in lack and limitation? Am I judgmental of others and their success? If so, I keep that energy for myself. Am I holding on to an old (or new) grudge or unforgiveness against anyone?"

If you don't release such energy, you frustrate the realization of your vision.

Sometimes we may be hiding these traits from ourselves, so we have to bring them to the surface.

One way to help bring these traits to our awareness is to practice mindful meditation. In this self-awareness practice, you observe your thoughts and see what bubbles up. It's amazing what you can be aware of when your mind is still and quiet. You become aware of the qualities that inhibit growth. You can make a new choice on what to hold on to and what to release.

However, if you don't have such awareness, you can't make a choice and will likely continue to do what you have always done.

Life (and death) is in the power of the tongue
Another way to help identify the qualities that we are consciously or unconsciously holding on to is to examine the words we use. They often give us a clue as to what we believe about ourselves and our world.

If a co-worker offers an idea for a project, and our response before we have a chance to research is "No way you can do that," that may be an indication that we may have a negative mindset that needs to be released.

Once you've identified such qualities, you can create a releasing statement to assure these traits are no longer running the show. For example, if you find one of the characteristics you are holding on to is lack and limitation, and you find yourself saying things like, "I can't afford to do that." You can say, "I release the idea there is not enough."

Such beliefs are incongruent with abundance, and the truth is, we live in a universe made up of endless ideas.

When I was a board member of a nonprofit spiritual community in Miami, Florida, we faced what appeared to be a crisis. We had a stack of bills. There is nothing wrong with having a pile of bills so long as you have a stack of money to pay them. Well, we didn't have a stack of cash.

To make things worse, while repairing the roof, the workers discovered asbestos. It was going to cost over $100,000 to remove the asbestos and make the building safe for the people to meet. We had to move out of the building and gather in a hotel until the removal of the asbestos.

In the meantime, we faced what seemed to be an impossible situation. There appeared to be no way we would be able to raise or borrow the money to remove the asbestos. When asked, "Does anyone believe there is a way out of this situation?" No one was ready to say yes.

Then one of the board members challenged us not to leave the room until we at least had an agreement that it was possible to come up with a way to solve the asbestos problem. One or two members half-heartedly said it was possible.

While in the room, the air conditioning went out. It was August, so it was hot. Then one of the members said, "Lock the doors and don't let anyone in, and don't let anyone out until we have an agreement that it is possible!" I don't know if he was joking about holding everyone hostage, but no one tried to leave.

And lo and behold, one by one, everyone chimed in and agreed that we could get the money needed to get rid of the asbestos. After the board meeting, one of the members went to a local bank. I don't know what he said, but apparently, he made an offer the bank officer could not refuse. Because, despite not meeting the standard lending requirements for getting a $100,000 loan, we got the money!

It all started because a group of people believed it was possible. There is power in belief.

Come out from Behind the Bushes

Sometimes we hide from ourselves.

One way we hide is by not bringing into the open or talking about the things we don't want others to know about us. These are secrets you'll take to your grave rather than reveal them to the world.

However, if you want to create the life you want, love, and deserve as well as come from a place of power and worthiness, you must be willing to share matters that stop you from unleashing your full potential. Specifically, they are matters that we are ashamed of, fearful about, or make us feel vulnerable.

If you are familiar with 12-step programs, after taking a fearless moral inventory, there is the fifth step. This step reads in part, "to admit to another human being the exact nature of our wrongs."

I'm a follower of the program and know many people get stuck at this step. They procrastinate like nobody's business before completing the fifth step.

Often this step includes secrets we are determined to die with us. Like many others, I put off facing this step for weeks before I finally walked through my self-created fears around sharing myself with another human being.

Once I did take the leap and shared my deepest secrets with my sponsor, I experienced an emotional release and high I did not anticipate.

A psychological, emotional, and spiritual clearing took place.

All kinds of opportunities opened up for me that I previously either did not see or were not available.

One of the most startling revelations was what I considered shameful, were not significant to any of the people I shared with—my sponsor and members of the 12 step group. I experienced those feelings only because I believed in their power.

That belief was holding me back from creating my best life.

What must you become?
You know it is within your potential to manifest your vision, but you are not moving in that direction. Sometimes you may cover it up and not bring to the light what needs to change in your life for that vision within you to spring forth.

So we ask the question: "What fears, perceived shame, or regrets must I face and bring to the light, so they no longer block the realization of my good?"

The vision is already complete in the mind of the "God Force." Just as the oak tree is already in the acorn, our vision is already inherently part of who we are. Our job is to create the conditions that make the manifestation of the idea inevitable.

We don't have to make it happen with our own will and power. Our job is to align with what has already happened. We do this by becoming the right people and radiating the right energy. This evolution requires we engage in fearless self-examination and ferret out those things that are hindering the vision.

Release, Release

To be our best selves is not a matter of adding anything to us. Instead, it is a matter of letting go and releasing those traits and qualities that do not serve us.

So we ask ourselves, "What traits do I have to let go of to make my vision come true?" Is it is selfishness? Envy of others? Are we putting other people down? When an obstacle shows up, do we automatically go to the worst possible outcome rather than ask, "What can I learn from this experience?" Anything along these lines doesn't do anything to anyone else but ourselves. We may think, on some level, what we feel about another person, group of people, or organization is doing something horrible to them. However, nothing is happening to anyone or anything outside of us. We keep the energy we send out.

There is a statement by Imelda Shanklin in her book, *What are You?*, in which she says, "Don't want for another person what you would not like to objectify in your own life." Whatever you send out, they get the copy; you keep the original.

Thus, in our meditation we observe, we hear, and listen to the answers to the question, "What is it that I must release to become what I need to be for the vision to be made real?

What must I embody?

Then you ask, "What qualities do I need to embody to assure I align with that vision that is within me?" Qualities include those needed to bring your vision forward in your personal life, a project you are working on for yourself, or goals for your organization. Is it courage? Do I need to be more of a risk-taker? Is it more self-discipline and intentional action? Is it perseverance?

In essence, you are asking yourself, "How must I grow to embody this vision? Are there any particular qualities I need to activate to help move this vision forward.

Then affirm that quality. Whether it is perseverance, not giving a hoot about what other people think, or understanding that some people criticize others as if there is some sort of prize in it. When it comes to dealing with criticisms from other people, you have to have the quality of not giving a you know what about what other people think.

Then take action that aligns with the quality you have chosen to embody. It's an action that helps create a new paradigm of being. You can't just talk about it.

What are Your Gifts?

Finally, to bolster the realization of your vision, ask, "What gifts do I have that will contribute to, help reveal, or glorify the vision?"

We all have gifts and talents. Sometimes we overlook them or dismiss them as small. To accelerate the development leverage of our vision, don't say, "I do not have enough talent. Instead, say, "I will use the talent that I have." When we use our God-given talent, the universe gives us an assist to help make our vision come true.

Finally, for all this to work, we have to have a willing attitude. All of us have been at points in our life when we have had that willingness. It starts by embodying the qualities needed to make the vision come alive in us.

Interestingly the spiritual work we do—affirmations, denials, or visualizations—is not directed toward the external vision. Instead, the work is to reveal the qualities we must have as part of our consciousness. Remember, the idea is already complete on the spiritual level. We are here to be the vessels through which the vision or plan manifests. The image does not depend on what's happening in the external environment. Instead, it happens through us as the walking vibration and instrumentality through which the vision will manifest.

Endogenous vs. Indigenous beings

That's why Ralph Waldo Emerson called us endogenous beings as opposed to indigenous. If a plant is indigenous, it can only grow in the correct or its natural environment.

As endogenous beings, we take our environment with us. We are both the environment for the vision and the vision itself. So our inner work is about creating the circumstances so the image can show up in the material form.

Once you are clear on the ideal vision for your life, it is time to anchor the image in your mind and body. For that to happen, you can do the following exercise:

1. Imagine the year has arrived in which your envisioned future has come true. It can be one year, three years, or five years in the future. Establish your timeline.
2. Imagine your future self is living this vision, and a top talk show host is interviewing you. The interviewer is asking you how you were able to reach your goals, and most importantly how do you feel today.
3. Imagine you are your future self speaking to the interviewer. Describe the positive emotions that you feel within every cell of your body. Feel the feeling right now when you picture that you are living your dream vision.
4. You describe it as it is happening now! Explain all the steps along the way that led you to get to the point where your future self is.

Your ideal vision reflects an accumulation of your typical days. Your perfect day is what you practice on a day to day basis. So in order to be those fit and vital instruments through which the vision comes through, we must practice certain habits on a day to day basis. We explore those habits in the next chapter.

Take Back Your Future! Practice # 3

To help turn your vision into reality once you're clear on what the vision for your life or project is:

1. Feel the vision with every fiber of your being.
2. Write down your vision and the supporting goals.
3. Read your vision two times a day—once in the morning and once before going to bed.
4. Take small action steps every day.
5. Start before you feel you're ready or before you have the "perfect plan" because there is no perfect plan.

Chapter 4

Set a Powerful Direction for Your Day – Daily Habits

I had a special older cousin named Gene Wright. He passed away some years ago from a debilitating illness. Before he made his transition, he asked me to officiate his memorial service. It was an honor I will always cherish.

Gene was a Navy man. When I was seven or eight years old, he taught me how to make a bed the Navy way. He took me through the steps of making the bed, including how to tuck the corners with military precision. The sheets had no slack, and you could bounce a quarter on them.

At the time, my cousin said to me, "When you make your bed, you lay the foundation for your day. It sets you in the right direction." I didn't know whether he was using that as a ruse to get me to make my bed every day, but it stuck with me. Consequently, I make my bed every day (well mostly), and it indeed helps set in motion the foundation for my day.

Making up a bed may seem a small achievement; but, making your bed a daily ritual does create a tone for the remainder of your day. According to Naval Admiral William McRaven, the former commander of the U.S. Special Operations, "If in the morning, you make your bed, you will have accomplished the first task of the day. It will give you a small sense of pride, and it will encourage you to do another task and another and another and another. By the end of the day, that one task completed will have turned into many tasks completed. Making your bend will reinforce the fact that little things in life matter."

Creating your best life is a matter of doing little things over and over again as you move in the direction of your goal.

Making your bed is just one practice that is key to setting an excellent foundation for a great day and, ultimately, a great life.

A study of very successful and accomplished people found that nearly all of them have morning rituals or habits to help lay the foundation for a successful day. If we create enough favorable days in a row, they eventually add up to a successful life.

Here are some rituals successful people do that are worth considering as a way to put your day on sound footing:

Every morning set your intention for the day. Such an aim can be how it is you want to show up throughout the day. You ask yourself, "What qualities do I want to radiate and demonstrate today?" "As you go through the day and encounter people, whether at work, the store, community meetings, with friends, what words would you want them to associate with you?" You probably don't want words like rude, grumpy, depressed, or hateful.

You may recall people who exuded such qualities. Most likely, they left you drained and depleted or just sucked the energy out of you.

Don't be one of those people.

Instead, ask yourself, "What words do I want people to use to describe me when I leave their presence?" Brainstorm and pick three words that you want to set up as an intention for how you want to show up. They might be words such as caring, reliable, considerate, patient, compassionate, joy-filled, or inspiring.

It's safe to say you want people who remember you to describe you by words like these. As part of your morning ritual, take three of these words and write them down or put them on your phone and set your alarm to go off three times a day to remind you how you want to show up that day.

Everyday Angela, my wife, took our son to school, she had him repeat positive words to live by before he got out of the car to start his school day. They were words about living a life of significance and making a difference. Those words set his intention for the day until it became part of his consciousness. It was a powerful ritual that set the direction of his life, and they can do the same for you. Moreover, when you begin to live showing up from a positive intention, it can uplift the lives of the people who cross your path.

When I lived in Miami, Florida, I use to take my clothes to a dry cleaner next to the development where I lived. Every Monday, I would usually drop off a bundle of clothes, and I would encounter the same gentleman who would take my bunch of clothes. His disposition was, to say the least, grumpy. Most of the time, it was outright negative and rude. How he stayed in business relating to his customers like that is a miracle in itself.

For some reason, I kept going back to that business. Coincidently, it was around the time I decided to set my intention on how I was going to show up when I encountered people. One of my words was "Upbeat." So every time I came to the counter of his cleaners and interacted with him, my conversation with him was always as positive and uplifting as I could make it.

Despite my upbeat interactions, his disposition was nonreactive at best and hostile at worse. But, I felt this would be good practice on how to show up based on my daily intention, regardless of how he responded.

There was a time I was away for a couple of months and did not go to the cleaners to drop off any clothes. When I came back, I got an unexpected greeting from my entrepreneurial friend.

He proclaimed, "Where have you been! I've been missing you. Every week I look forward to you coming by so I can see and talk with you. I feel so much better when you are around."

I had no idea I was having any effect on him. I sure couldn't tell by his response. It just goes to show the power of living from your intention for how you show up.

Pick three such qualities. They can be peace, joyous, positive, helpful, patient, etc. And then no matter what you face throughout the day, seek to bring these qualities to life. The more you set such an intention, the more those qualities will become part of your way of being each day.

Give Yourself a Mental Cleanse with Morning Pages

Another great ritual you can use every morning is a practice called morning pages. I was introduced to this ritual by Julia Cameron, author of *The Artists Way* when I attended a conference in Santa Fe, New Mexico.

Here's how the ritual goes. Every morning write three pages in longhand. Write whatever rises to the top of mind no matter what it is. Don't overthink it and write without taking your pen off the paper. If you can't think of anything, write "I can't think of anything" until something pops in your mind. As you are writing, you may think, "This is crazy," or, "This is just a stupid waste of time." If that's what comes to mind, write that down.

When you practice this ritual, something amazing will happen. Not only will you become more aware of the thoughts that are passing through your mind, but you will also find yourself more emotionally centered.

Your self-awareness will skyrocket so you can see yourself with greater clarity, and you'll begin to observe the scores of stuff that is showing up in your mind you may not have been conscious of before. With such awareness, you can make new choices on how you see yourself, what thoughts you want to release, and what ideas to replace.

Morning pages allow you to dump all the debris and make way for more constructive and creative thinking. You will be able to silence your biggest enemy—that inner critic and the "I'm not good enough syndrome."

Moreover, by practicing this ritual, you will become less anxious as those feelings are faced, written down, and eventually released. You will also let go of other negative emotions, whether it be envy, fear, feelings that lead to procrastination, and vulnerability.

All those emotions can be put on paper and seen for the illusions they are. When bringing that negative stuff to the light and look at it face to face, it loses its power. You realize it is not as big as you may have made them be, and you take your control back.

Meditation

Of course, the mother of all rituals is the practice of some form of meditation. I recall asking what I considered to be a very enlightened person about his meditation practice.

He responded by saying he started his day with thirty minutes of meditation first thing in the morning. Then every hour on the hour, he goes into silence for 5 minutes. Before going to bed at night, he would review his day by asking himself, "What worked?" "What could I have done better?" and meditating on the question, "What can I do tomorrow to be a better person than I was today?"

I reacted by saying, "You'd have to be superhuman to do something like that every day!"

His response to me was quite enlightening as he said, "Anyone not making meditation practice a part of their day is superhuman! Can you imagine trying to get through the day with trying to climb the ladder of success, heal your body temple, solving the litany of problems you face daily, or getting with the right people to make your business a success? He went further to say, "If anyone is doing that without a meditation practice to keep grounded, that would be superhuman!"

We don't want to rely on our might, power, and wits to get through the day. We want to be super-spiritual while we go through this human experience allowing this "something" that is greater than ourselves to serve as the wind beneath our wings.

There is power in meditation. It can help us navigate our day and our lives more effectively, efficiently, and peacefully. Mahatma Gandhi said once when he had so much on his plate, "I have so much to do, I need to meditate two hours a day instead of one." Such is the power of meditation in life.

Dr. Martin Luther King Jr., when asked as he reflected on what he had done in his short life what he would have done differently said, "I would have spent more time meditating."

Tim Ferris, author of the book, Tools of Titans,[7] discovered more than 80% of successful world-

____

[7] Tim Ferris, Tools of Titans, The Tactics, Routines, and Habits of Billionaires, Icons and World-Class Performers, 2016

class performers had a meditation practice and it cultivated their ability to be in the present moment and not react to the disruptive events that pop up in their day to day living. They ranged from elite athletes to writers and everyone in between.

Meditation is a skill that anyone can learn and can improve everything you do.

Don't leave home without it.

Take Back Your Future! Practice #4

To lay a great foundation for your day, choose at least one of the following practices and commit to following it every morning.

1. Meditate for a minimum of twenty minutes.

2. Pick one word that reflects how you will show up throughout the day. Write it down so you can see it periodically as you go through your day, or put the word in your phone so it pops up as an hourly reminder.

3. Write three pages, longhand, of everything that pops in your mind. Write without judgment or self-criticism.

Chapter 5

Up-Level Your Energy

In 1985, I was in a drug rehabilitation center called Concept House.

Although it was a humdrum, nondescript building in a part of Miami called Little Haiti, it was arguably one of the best centers in South Florida. What made it so was not only its programming and structure but the counselors and instructors who worked there. One of the instructors was a gentleman named Ralph Malloy. Ralph was one of the students that got kicked out of Harvard in the 1960s because he participated in LSD experiments with Timothy Leary.

Ralph was a brilliant therapist who earned two doctorate degrees. He was also a therapist to actors, including a local television star from the TV show Miami Vice—one of the hottest shows on television at the time. Ralph didn't need to be working at this rehab center but had recovered from heroin addiction and went through his rehabilitation years prior. When I was at Concept House, he facilitated the encounter and reality groups; this was his way of giving back and paying it forward.

When I entered Concept House, I had a great deal of guilt as a result of what I perceived I had done to my life. Everything I valued in my life, I lost. I believed I would never be able to get my life back on track again. This feeling of guilt drained my energy, and I wasn't able to get out of the haze I found myself in on a day to day basis. I was getting plenty of sleep and was eating healthy. But this draining of energy would not go away.

As part of my rehab, I had to address my inability to forgive myself. I was beating myself up for the life missteps I had made along the way. I didn't think it would ever go away. Every day for the first two months that I was in Concept House, I would, in some way, try to shake myself of the guilty feelings I was carrying.

It wasn't for the lack of trying. I did everything that the center offered. I discussed my feelings of guilt with my counselor during my one-on-one sessions with him. I shared during my group sessions. I undertook Gestalt Therapy in which I play-acted by confronting myself. Nothing seemed to work.

Then one day, I woke up, and all the guilt I was carrying disappeared. It seemed like a miracle. I kept looking over my shoulder to see if it would somehow come back. But it never did.

I had finally forgiven myself. There was a surge of energy within me that I had not experienced for quite some time.

What stuck with me was the surge of energy. And man, what a difference it made to have my power back; it helped me move forward in my life.

I bring up energy because it takes a lot of energy to create the level of success you want in life—whatever success happens to mean to you. Without get up and go, you won't go very far. You need that enthusiasm to bolster and maintain the stamina necessary to do the work and perform the tasks for your vision. As the saying goes, ideas don't work unless you do.

Forgiveness is one of the practices that one must undertake to have that energy. When you're in a state of resentment toward yourself or anyone else, it not only blocks your blessings, it drains your energy. Plus, if you attempt to create a magnificent dream and your mind is full of energy of resentment, guilt, or anger, it will choke out that dream.

To create the life you want, you must have energy and enthusiasm for what you are doing. Don King, the famous or infamous (depending on your perspective) boxing promoter, was asked, "What is the secret of your success?" He responded that it was energy and enthusiasm because if you set yourself on fire, people will come from miles around to watch you burn.

We must be burning with energy and enthusiasm to manifest the visions of our life. One way to assure we are not hindering, blocking, or obstructing our zeal, is to practice the art and science of forgiveness.

There are other things we can do to ensure we have the energy, vitality, and vigor to create our best lives now. We not only want vibrant emotional energy (which forgiveness aides) but vibrant mental and physical energy.

When someone has the energy and vibrancy, the more likely they will be able to create the life they want rather than settle for the life you have.

Emotional Energy

No doubt practicing for forgiveness—both toward others and ourselves—clears up our energy field so our natural vibrancy flows from us. There is something else we need to be aware of and practice that will add to our energy field, and that's to be careful of the words we use. We can cause energy leakages whenever we engage in meaningless conversations.

Often through the course of the day, we may find ourselves in conversations that have no meaning. When we participate in such discussions, we already know what the end is going to be even before we start because there is nothing more than opinions going back and forth. There is no real dialogue going on because everyone is just maintaining their positions, staying the same, and trying to change the other person's point of view. Yet, for some reason, many people remain in such conversations anyway.

Then at the end of the day, we may wonder why we are so tired that all we can do is fall into the bed. Our energy is sapped because we have allowed the leakage of this cosmic force through meaningless conversation. The conversation becomes even more pointless when we're getting in other people's business by trying to figure out what someone is doing in their life. Such talk erodes our energy.

Instead, we want to engage in authentic dialogue with other people. Genuine dialogue is always about the expansion of our consciousness and perception about life. In a real conversation, we're not tossing around opinions in which we are posturing why "I'm right, and you're wrong." After a while, it just gets old as well as drain our energy.

I invite you to eavesdrop a little bit and become aware of the conversations that are taking place around you. You'll discover they just go around in circles, and there is no real resolution. There is no looking at the issue from a higher point of view from either party. There are no lofty ideas or ideals addressed. It's a form of the walking dead. To keep your energy and vitality high, we don't want to be part of that. Alternately, we want to prevent our power from being dissipated with the frivolity of meaningless conversations.

Dream Castling

Instead, we want to up-level our energy field by engaging in a practice known as "Dream

Castling." When we Dream Castle, we focus our attention and imagination on talking about the "great possibilities" in life. We do so without censoring it or putting qualifications around it or doubting it in any way. For example, you say to yourself or anyone who will play with you, things like, *"Wouldn't it be wonderful to fly to Egypt and explore the pyramids"*; *"How great it would be to have a business that I love and be able to live anywhere in the world?"*; *"Wouldn't it be wonderful to go to Paris and see clothes I designed at the "Paris Fashion Week" fashion show."*; *"How magnificent would it be to gather up all my extended family for a reunion on Fiji Island!"* or *"How great would it be to be the best-selling author I've always wanted to be?"*.

Whatever lights up your soul, speak into that, and you will have an uplift in energy.

When lifted into that energy field, you're not hindered by the doubts that arise with questions like, "How am I going to do that?" You're in the zone of possibilities. Your job is to know the **"*what*."** Because when it is yours to do, the **"*how*"** will reveal itself.

When you are in that space, you lift your liveliness, and the lesser energy does not dissipate your belief in what's possible. As we stay in that energy, the universe will move you to the right place, or the course of history will change for you. This friendly universe will become whatever is necessary for the dream that is within you to come out.

When I was in high school, I attended a summer debate camp at Georgetown University in Washington, D.C. My debate partner and I had finished our junior year and we were fortunate enough to receive a scholarship to attend. It was a big deal since James Unger, the premier collegiate debate coach from the 1960s through the 1980s, ran the camp.

In contrast to the inner-city school that my partner and I attended, most of the high school participants attended private or elite public schools. The fact we didn't attend a private or elite public school didn't hinder our success. By the end of our junior year, we were one of the top debater teams in Miami Dade County, Florida.

While attending the camp, I happened to mention to some of the other participants I wanted to go to Harvard University. One of the students, knowing my background, finances, and how difficult it was to get accepted into that school, said it would never happen. He was trying to enroll me in his limited belief. However, I didn't buy into his idea about me, my station in life, or how impossible he thought my vision was. I stayed in the field of possibilities.

I held my vision. And while I got on the waiting list at Harvard, I was ultimately accepted into Princeton University (I later learned of an inside joke by Princeton students and alumni that says compared to Princeton, Harvard is a good trade school).

As I look back, I realize that in my **naiveté**, I was not concerned about the facts or my history or how it was going to happen. I just focused on the "**what**," and whatever was needed to make it happen showed up. For example, I got a sterling letter of recommendation from my English teacher who happened to have received the honor of National Teacher of the Year. I could not have made that happen on my own. But things like this happen when you stay in the field of possibilities.

Speak Words That Uplift You

There is a statement in Proverbs that says, "Man's curses fall and surround him like his cloak." Curses are those things that suppress our true essence. And it is not anyone else doing it to us; we do it to ourselves through our self-talk. Sometimes we are so hard on ourselves. What we say to ourselves is cursing the infinite Spirit that is within us. Ultimately those words serve as our cloak that influences our physical body as well as our life experiences. So we want to discipline ourselves, not to beat ourselves up or harshly speak to ourselves for whatever mistakes we think we have made.

The reality is that from the universe's perspective, there aren't any mistakes, only feedback. Just as an actor when he or she makes a ***miss take*** in rehearsal, we have the opportunity for a do-over. We get more chances to get it right. So rather than speak to ourselves harshly for our missteps and thus deplete our energy, we see life as a research project where we are researching the art of successfully failing. We are finding ways that something did not work out and thus getting us closer to finding what will work out. We keep our energy field high.

Moreover, we always have the power of choice to look at every event that happens in our life experience and name it excellent, magnificent, or wisdom making. We see it as a research project.

Daily Checklist to Up-Level Your Energy

In addition to removing emotional blockages such as forgiveness to boost your energy level, there are overarching researched guidelines that will boost your physical energy. The following is a list of suggested guidelines:[8]

- When you take on tasks or work during the day, take a break every 50 to 60 minutes. Get up, walk around, and hydrate your body. These breaks will sharpen your mental focus when you go back to what you are doing.
- Sleep at least 8 hours each night. If there are days you can't meet that goal, take a short nap. It will do wonders to give you more energy.
- Drink a minimum of eight 8 ounce glasses of water.

---

[8] Note these are just suggested guidelines. Make sure you consult your health care professional before making changes to either your diet or exercise routines.

- Exercise 3-5 times per week. It can be a 30 to 45-minute walk each time.
- Practice "breath scaling" 3 times a day. Breath scaling is an escalating series of breaths in which you breathe faster and deeper. This exercise helps cleanse and energize the body.
- Hug a lot.
- Eat meals with lots of greens, preferably organic plant-based foods.
- Take a multi-vitamin supplement for Omega 3 fish oil, calcium, and vitamins.
- Limit eating starch-based and processed foods.

Take Back Your Future! Practice #5

Holding on to resentment or judgment toward yourself or others inhibits your natural energy flow. To generate energy, you must release the baggage of a past experience. This happens through the practice of forgiveness. Here are steps you can use to forgive:

1. Be aware of the need to forgive.
2. Be **_willing_** to forgive.
3. Ask the Universe or "The Force", Spirit, or whatever you call Universal Intelligence for help and guidance.
4. Face and totally feel your feelings.
5. Accept full responsibility for your feelings without blaming or judging anyone else.
6. Surrender the results.
7. Repeat steps 2-6 as often as necessary.
8. Be patient with yourself.

The above steps are essentially the same for self-forgiveness work.

Chapter 6

Go from Idea to Reality - Beyond the Law of Attraction to the Law of Action

Ideas, Ideas. There are so many. Too many to count. But it does no good to draw insights from the Ideasphere unless we bring those ideas into manifestation or make them a reality. If you're like me, you've probably had lots of great (or not so great) ideas. But the question is, "Are we able to make these ideas happen?"

During my previous life as an attorney, a friend and I came up with a plan for an educational board game. We made the prototype and tested it with a few kids we knew. It seemed like a great idea. Right off the bat, we had a tremendous amount of enthusiasm for the project as well as illusions of grandeur.

Since we planned to introduce the game to local schools, we met with a school board member. He was open to the idea, but not overly enthusiastic. I sensed he knew this was going require a lot of effort to bring this idea to fruition.

Not only were we going to have to navigate the political terrain for this game to have a chance after testing the game, but we'd also have to find a company to produce the game. Then we'd have to figure out distribution and marketing. That's on top of figuring out the right price point for the game, and gearing up support staff to help with the details of the project as we continued to deal with the overall planning necessary to make this project a success.

At first, enthusiasm and the adrenalin for the project was at a fever pitch. But after that initial rush of excitement waned, we reached a mental plateau. We started to get distracted by the distractions that inevitably crop up.

Today, such distractions may include binging on a TV series that you missed and is now on Netflix. Or when you should be focusing on the project that you had so much passion for, you end up going to the store to buy something you do not need.

Or maybe, you drop the idea you've been working on to pursue the next new idea or shiny object that captures your fancy.

Unable to bring an idea to reality and make it happen is why so many people have half-baked projects. But to create your best life, you can't just attract a Divine Idea and leave it at the idea stage. The goal is to bring the idea into expression in the three-dimensional world.

For that to happen, we move from the law of attraction to the law of action. After all, the master teacher Jesus noted when his antagonists wanted to persecute him for working on the Sabbath, "*The Father is working, and I also am working.*"[9]

Spirit has done its part by giving us the idea, but we have to continue the process by bringing the concept into reality.

Make your cherished Ideas Real

So let's say you have the ideas from the Ideasphere. It's a big idea, and you know it has merit. Now, what do you do on a day to day basis to make the idea a reality? What are practical things you can do to finish what you want to finish, see it happen, and

---

[9] John 5:17, New Revised Standard Version

work along with the principle that the Universe is working, so I too must work along with it?

Let's start what is often the typical way to get things done but usually does not work and needs to be released as soon as possible.

It's the to-do lists that seem to go on and on. To-do lists are great at keeping most of us busy but don't help bring into reality our most important priorities.

I can relate.

I recall my days as a manager in training at the Miami Herald circulation department, as a CEO, and before that, the leader of a spiritual community in Miami, Florida. I did a lot of busy work but did not always get the results I wanted. I would sometimes have a list of 20 or more tasks to do, knowing full well I couldn't do them all.

I'd end up doing what was pressing and urgent rather than what was most important to complete my most important priorities. I felt rushed, overwhelmed, and believed there was never enough time to get the essential things done.

Then I was reminded of the 80 - 20 rule, also known as Pareto's Law. This principle says that 80%

of our results come from 20% of our effort and time. Conversely, 80% of our labor produces only 20% of our results. Our to-do lists, more often than not, end up being in that 80% that provides that measly 20%.

To not get stuck getting that 20% result, the key is to focus on the few things that move the big projects forward and to ignore the rest. It's easy to get caught up in an avalanche of minutiae and feel rushed all the time. But the lack of time simply means we have not prioritized effectively. It's time to stop and ask, "What the heck am I doing?"

Getting It Done

There is a tactic that works and will do wonders for you if you stick to it. It will get you focused, eliminate overwhelm, and make the most important things you want to see happen, happen.

The key is to come up with 1. A to-do list, and 2. A not-to-do list.

The to-do list should only include those 20% things that support your purpose and vision for your life. To bring this into focus for you and help you get there, imagine you had a health condition in which you could only work two hours a day if you wanted to stay alive—no exceptions.

You might be saying, "that's impossible." Or "no way I could just work two hours a day." If someone told you that it is possible to function with just 4-5 hours of sleep a night, you would not believe it. But new mothers do it all the time.

By focusing on the essential 20%, you will identify the critical areas in your life that are truly important: business, personal, health, relationships, leisure, etc. Particularly as they relate to and support your reason for doing what you do.

Then turn those essential things you do into projects. Every idea you come up with, anything you work on, is a project.

Here is where you go to the image of your vision and pull out key projects that support it. One critical project of my picture of the future was writing this book to encourage people to experience their best life now. It was and is a pivotal project to help me fulfill that intention.

Your projects might cover areas such as Business, Personal, Health, Relationships.

It does not matter if your projects are personal or work-related; you have to treat each one as its project.

For example, are you planning a party to recognize long-time volunteers for your organization? That's a project.

Or maybe you have to present a vital sales pitch on Friday. That's a project.

Perhaps you want to write your book. That's a project if there ever was one.

Each project started as an idea. The ideas are what you want to see completed. Such aims, as I noted, are not just work-related, although they can be. They also can be getting in shape to lose X number of pounds. Or raising money for a nonprofit you support and where you volunteer.

You have to consider these non-work related activities as projects. If you don't, you will underestimate how much time and energy you have to work on the remaining projects

Then on the top of a sheet of paper lengthwise create five columns and type or write a heading for each column

Highest - High - Medium - Low - Idle / These represent the priority levels of each of your identified projects.

It would look something like this:

Action Steps in One List

Action Item		Project	Due Date
Identify Agent for Book		Personal	17 - Aug
Set up meeting w Sales Rep		XYZ Co	18 - Aug
Pick up costumes for Mtg		Personal	19- Aug
Finalize PowerPoint for Mtg		Co	21-Aug
Have recording of Mtg Transcribed		XYZ CO	29-Aug
Update LinkedIn Page		Personal	3-Sept

To help keep order, you can create a file for each project and put the data in an expanded folder with a list of the projects on the front of the expanded folder as a visual reminder. Once you have identified your aims, break done each project into its main components.

The components are action steps, resources, parking lot.

Of these components, **action steps are hands down the most important**. In fact, if you don't do anything but follow through on the action steps, you will experience and create your best life now.

If you don't have action steps, there will be no action. And if there is no action, there is no creation, and if there is no creation, there is no best life for you.

So, what are action steps? They are tasks that are specific and concrete that you must do or delegate to someone else to move the project forward to their completion.

Someone has to own the step—either you or the person you have delegated the task to.

Start each step with a verb. For example:

1. Design invitations for the awards banquet.

2. Write the first draft of the letter.

3. Place deposit on the hall for the awards banquet.

There will be times that you have to wait for someone to complete a step or follow up with them. Make this an action step. For example, "Ensure Marion has signed the banquet hall contract."

Whenever or wherever an action step reveals itself, capture it. Not just at meetings. It may come up in a phone call or a lunch conversation. If it's needed to make the project happen, write it down.

Resources

Resources aren't things you take action on. They can be notes, ideas from meetings, or handouts you've gotten from workshop or class. They are there simply for you to possibly refer to in the future.

Parking *lot*

Ideas that pop up from time to time but not something you will take action on now but may in the future. They are new ideas that come up but are not relevant to the project or main projects you are working on right now.

For example, you may have an excellent idea for a speech or an article that you want to happen in the future. It's not something you are going to do right now, but later on, you might. You capture the idea because you will forget the idea if you don't.

Trust me, you will forget. Sometimes ideas come to me in dreams, so I have a note pad near the bed so I can write them down as soon as I wake up. Otherwise, they just seem to disappear into the ethers. Once you capture them, they may lead to other ideas or projects further down the line

By focusing on action steps, resources, and parking lot items, you simplify your process. You won't get lost in the different aspects of the project. You're zeroing in on these three areas. But your primary focus will be on the action steps. It is the action steps that will move you to creating what you want and desire in life.

Put all your action steps across all projects on one list, so you're not jumping from one record to the next. You can use an excel spreadsheet where you identify the action, the project, and the due date. You can highlight critical items in one color and completed tasks in another

Every day, make sure you are working on your highest and high priorities. Work on at least one of these priorities every day and during your most productive energy cycle of the day. Block out that time. For me, it's 5:30 a.m. to 8 a.m. before I leave for the office. For others, it's late at night. I know one very productive creator who does his best work between 10:00 p.m. and 5 a.m.

Whatever works for you, do it.

Slay the productivity vampires

The vampires of productivity are everywhere. They come disguised as emails and social media. At one time, it was mostly TV. If you spend 3 hours a day on TV (whether it's Netflix, HBO, or watching cat videos on YouTube) for 21 hours per week, those hours add up to 1092 hours over a year. If you do that for twenty years, you end up losing 21,980 hours or 2, 730 days. Now with tablets, smartphones, and minitablets, there are even more insidious time suckers and productivity destroyers.

Remember, time is precious. Once you lose it, you can never get it back. Respect time.

Time is your most precious resource when it comes to what's needed to get things done and to make your ideas happen.

What's the solution? Let's start with emails.

Most emails are what other people want you to do to help carry out their agenda. One of the best tactics to handle emails is to not answer emails in the morning (unless it's part of your job description). Once you start answering emails at the start of your day, it's easy to get sucked down a rabbit hole of no return. A lot of people think you are just waiting at your computer so you can answer their email the instant you receive it.

Don't fall for it.

To address the email dilemma, set aside 30 minutes to answer emails before lunch and 30 minutes before leaving the office. Better yet, pick an hour during your least productive time of day (say an hour before leaving) to answer emails and let folks know that's when you respond to emails. Also, let the senders know that if it is an urgent matter to text you. Most of the time, nothing is that urgent, and the issue can wait.

Of course, as I noted, if your job depends on answering emails - for example, you are in customer service- by all means, answer the emails. However, most people don't have to do this as part of their job

When it comes time to address emails, prioritize two types:

1. People who you are waiting for to complete an action to meet your top projects.

2. People you need to assist you in moving your projects forward.

All other emails you can delegate to someone else, address after completing your action list, or let them go.

It's easy to get caught up in busywork. Busywork is redoing your to-do list, making unnecessary calls on a whim, or reading stuff that has nothing to do with getting what you need to get your task done. Of course, lying in wait is the most devious detraction—surfing the internet.

You must focus on the actions that support your most important projects.

As you go through your day, every couple of hours ask yourself two questions:

"Am I just being busy, or am I productive on my key projects?"

"Am I just making up stuff to do to avoid what matters?"

These questions will help you get focused and get you to eliminate activity for activity's sake.

Super Leverage Your Effort

If you want to supercharge your action and make your ideas happen, go on a media fast. Start with a week. For it to work, go cold turkey. You do it like pulling off a Band-Aid, do it quickly. Otherwise, you'll just get sucked in when you say: "Well, I'll just go on the web for a minute."

Trust me; it won't be for just a minute.

If you want to go back and wallow in an overflow of information after a week, go right ahead. But if you go on information fasts, the earth will continue to spin on its axis, and it will still revolve around the sun. So for five days, seven if you're daring:

- No newspapers, magazines, or audio stuff. Music is okay, however.

- Drop all news websites.
- Remember, no TV, except for an hour of pleasure viewing in the evening.
- Cut down on fact-based books. Fiction is okay. Books of fiction and fantasy help put the day behind you.
- No web surfing other than what you need to do to get your action list done.

Temptations will arise. Resist. Hold on. You can do it. Use your extra time to speak to your partner or spouse, talk to your kids, or spend that time meditating.

Now, if you must have a news fix, during lunch and not minute before, ask a colleague or waiter, "Anything important happen in the news today?" I haven't been able to check the news. As soon as you find the information doesn't affect you at all, stop. You will discover that most of the daily news has no relevance to you or your life at all.

There was a time I went to Nigeria, Africa, for ten days, and I didn't keep up with any news. Life was fine. I got caught up on the one or two things that might have been important, and life went on.

Power of Delegation

When doing your task or action items, ask yourself, "Is this something I can delegate?" Particularly, ask this question if you are doing something you do not enjoy or do poorly. One technique to help with this delegation process is to do the following:

1. Take a sheet of paper and draw a line down the middle.
2. On one side, write at the top "Things only I can do." On the other column, write" Things I can delegate."

You'll be pleasantly surprised at how many tasks you are doing that someone else can do for you.

I won't go into detail, but you can outsource many tasks you may be doing as you work on your projects. You can outsource tasks such as websites, brochures, editing, transcribing, logo creation, and book covers to online freelance platforms such as Upwork. Another similar company is called Fiverr. These companies represent a worldwide labor pool in which you can post a task you want done, and you will connect with freelancers from all over the world who can do the work for you. They tell you what it will cost, and you can check out their work, and see how much money they have made. You can even find out their customer ratings.

So those are a few tips to help you make your ideas a reality.

Some final thoughts on manifesting your ideas

As I bring this chapter to a close, I want to leave you some parting words of advice from someone who has tried and failed and tried again and learned what works along the way:

- Stay in the energy field and read your vision at least two times a day. Once in the morning and once before you go to sleep at night.
- Remain connected to the source by maintaining a consistent meditation practice. Remember, there is power in silence and going apart. Meditate at least 20 minutes in the morning. And do it consistently. The consistency is more important than the length of time you do it each day.
- Each year take at least a week in which you can go somewhere and do not do anything but be with yourself. It can be a silent retreat

or a place where you can get away and get in tune with nature.

- Continuously bombard yourself with positive information and people. Toxic people do not deserve your time. You deserve the best. To think otherwise is to be cruel to yourself. So be gentle with yourself. When you make a mistake, know it is just a miss-take. Just like an actor on set has a miss-take when reciting his or her lines, they can do it again. And so can you.

- When challenges come up, talk to yourself and say, "It's going to be alright." Ask yourself, "How many ways can this turn out in my favor? "Remember, the quality of the questions you ask, determine the quality of the answers you get.

Take Back Your Future! Practice #6

<u>Push Goals</u>

Push goals or projects make all other goals and projects easier to accomplish and give you a great sense of achievement. To take advantage of push goals:

1. Choose that one project that would make all other projects or goals easier to happen.

2. To help you select that goal or project ask, "If there is only one project I could accomplish, what would it be?" Select that goal.

3. Use a technique called "Back Tracking". Go to a place where you have no distractions and where you cannot be disturbed. Stay there for as many days as you can.

4. While at the distraction-free zone place, look back on all your past experiences to find out what you have learned.

5. Then look forward in time in which you see your completed project or goal. Identify every detail you can imagine that is necessary to complete the project.

6. Mentally walk back every step along the way.

7. Make these the steps you follow to successfully complete the project or meet the goal.

Chapter 7

Leave a Legacy - Live your Life as an Ancestor

In February 1998, I took my first trip to Africa. It was to Ghana, the western region of the continent. I flew from Miami, Florida to accompany a group of folks from Brooklyn, New York who were the sponsors of the trip.

The airline was Air Afrique. In addition to being excited about making the trip, there were two things I distinctly remember. One was the colorful African garb worn by the airline attendants. The second was when the pilots let me and a couple of other people visit the cockpit as we flew over the Atlantic Ocean. This was pre 911, so unless I become a commercial airline pilot, I doubt that's ever going to happen again.

While on the trip, one of the searing memories I have from the journey was my visit to the slave castles and 'the door of no return.' The door of no return was a portal through which enslaved people passed through after they were ripped from their families. They were then lowered into small boats and packed like cattle onto the larger ships that were sitting further out in the ocean. To go through the door of no return, meant a final goodbye to the freedom they knew and a horrifying journey across the sea.

Needless to say, for me and for many of the others I was with, it was an anguishing experience. Emotions ran the gamut of anger, despair, sadness, as well as feelings I could not identify at the moment. It was as if we could feel the presence and hear the echoes of the screams of the spirits of those human beings who went through the door. It left everyone present, including myself, in stunned silence.

Later that day, I, along with the rest of the group, went to the city of Accra to be part of the Akan Traditional Naming Ceremony. This was facilitated by the Chief Elder of the village. At the end of the ceremony, the Elder gave me my Ghanaian name, "*Kwami Tumase*". Kwame is the day of the week I was born. Tumase is a name that honors the elders in the village.

When the ceremony ended, I was invited to the Chief's Palace. During my conversation with the Elder, I shared my slave castle experience. I let him know the emotions we all went through when we faced 'the door of no return.'

The Elder Chief then gave me a perspective that caused me to view the experience in a new way. He explained that time does not exist. All and life happens simultaneously. That means that a "future" life can influence a "past" life as well as the other way around.

Because there is constant interaction between all lives, our life influences other beings, whether "future" or "past." Consequently, if we do something beneficial in this life, all people are affected. So the Elder said this to me, "If you live your life with the high positive energy, you will not only set in motion positive energy for future generations, you will renew and replenish past lives. When you send positive energy from the present, *your ancestors are freed up as well!*"

He went on to say, "This is what your ancestors expect from you. This is why you are here. It is stored in your DNA, and you are here to see new possibilities. Your ancestors went through what they did so that future generations will spread a new consciousness. When you do, they will be liberated along the way."

This idea is not only relevant to my experience with how I related to my Slave Castle experience, but it also applies to all of our experiences. That's because we are all interconnected. What affects one of us affects all of us—past, present, and future.

There are many challenges that we face in our world today. Wars and rumors of wars, climate crisis, and a sense of separation between people based on race, religion, ethnicity, or political party. But there are signs of hope.

One Friday evening, I dropped by a program called "Voices Unheard," the inaugural event founded by an organization called Emerging Wisdom. The gathering was composed primarily of millennials who came together to share their music, art, spoken word, and consciousness. The proceeds of the event went to support CARA, an organization dedicated to providing legal aid to the kids and parents separated from one another as a result of the controversial zero-tolerance immigration policy in 2018.

Although not directly related to the affected children and parents, the young people who organized the event believed they are nonetheless interconnected with them. They agreed to stand in support of them because it was a spiritual, moral, as well as a humanitarian concern. As a result, they felt they could not sit idly by without doing something to support their fellow human beings. They believed that as a human family, we can and should do better.

What struck me most was the organizers of the event recognized that if we are going to create a world that works for all and if we are to appreciate, and indeed celebrate all of humanity, we cannot live in isolation. We cannot just be concerned with ourselves.

We are one in Spirit and here to contribute to the Divine Plan that reflects the higher order of our being. For that to happen, we must be willing to go beyond the small self. To paraphrase a scriptural statement, if you try to save your little life, you'll l lose it; but if you lose your life (not think only of yourself) for the sake of the collective good, you'll experience what it means to have life eternal.

We are here to not just focus on the individual self but also serve as instruments of this spiritual presence so we can leave something magnificent behind for all of humanity. As we do, we live our lives as ancestors who contribute to the upliftment of humanity.

This is called legacy living. It is living with the understanding that one day all of us will leave something behind. Others are going to look back and notice what we have left behind. With this realization, we can live our life knowing that those who follow us can step into a positive vibrational wake.

Knowing this, we can choose to leave behind a vibrational stepladder that others can build on. That stepladder can be one of harmony, goodness, beauty, cooperation, and the possibilities of the human Spirit. If that is the legacy we individually and collectively leave, the people who follow us will have a higher likelihood to live the divine ideas and ideals of Spirit.

One person who knows the importance of legacy living is Greta Thunberg. In August 2018, Greta wanted world leaders to take action to address the climate crisis. She believed it's more than an emergency, and instead, a five-alarm fire.

Greta, who was fifteen years old at the time, started a student strike every Friday. She sat outside the Swedish parliament building in Stockholm to raise awareness about climate change.

The first few Fridays were lonely. During those beginning stages, it was only her and a few friends who participated. Greta sat down in front of the parliament building with a handwritten sign that said, "School strike for climate."

Fifteen months later, Greta's little-known strike evolved into inspiring millions of people, mostly youth, across the planet to participate in the Climate Strike March.

When she was interviewed by Reuters News, Greta stated, "*We have only been born into the world, we are going to have to live with this crisis our whole lives. So will our children and grandchildren and coming generations. We are not going to accept this. We are striking because we want a future, and we are going to carry on.*"

In our own way, we, too, can engage in legacy living. It's about living a life such that you leave behind something beneficial, beautiful, and even magnificent. It is something we bequeath to your ancestors, or our ancestors give to us.

I don't know if Greta and those who were part of the Emerging Wisdom group would describe what they were part of in such terms as legacy living. But no doubt, they were doing their part to contribute to a positive legacy. And that's a good thing.

Take Your Future Back! Practice #7

It helps to understand who we want to be during our lives and the legacy we want to leave by considering how we will be remembered after we're gone.

The fact of the matter is, life has an end date and we should want to make the most of our life as possible.

This exercise, writing your own obituary, will help you get clear on how to live the life your heart longs for. For many, talking about our own death is sensitive and uncomfortable. Despite our feelings about death, no one gets out of this life alive. In any event, when you do the exercise, you will find it extremely powerful.

Doing this exercise will help you live so when you look back over your life, there will be no regrets.

To write your obituary, answer the following questions:

1. What did I stand for when things got tough?
2. What were the decisions I made about the direction of my life that I'm proud of?
3. What were the top accomplishments I achieved?

a. At the ages 40, 50, 60, 70, 80?
4. What did the choices I made say about what matters to me?
5. How will I be remembered?
6. How will people remember me? Why?
7. Who did I care for?
8. What was I known to be interested in and passionate about?
9. What was my legacy

When you write your obituary, aim high and think big. Be inspired by what you write. While the words should reflect your true essence and not your ego, make sure they represent what you want, love, and deserve during your lifetime.

Chapter 8

Hijacking Your Life Back

Fast forward 30 years...

It was just another routine day until I got home from work...and my mother called. It was only then that I discovered she hadn't forsaken and deserted me. She had been desperately searching and hoping for 30 years, just as I had for 30 years. She had experienced 30 years of fear, angst, and desperation, just as I had. For three decades we had been two lost souls, hoping against hope, for a reunion of the mother/child relationship that had been stolen from us both.

Here's the picture of the two of us together.

It turns out my mother didn't just up and leave and decide never to return to my sister and me. Her and my father had a strained relationship and she needed to hit the pause button, to try and pull herself together. But unbeknownst to her, my father suddenly moved us from New York to Miami, and told everyone in the neighborhood that we were going to California. This was before the Internet and social media. It wasn't as easy to track people down unless you had a lot of money to hire a private detective.

However, this did not stop my mother from trying to find her children. For years, to no avail, she attempted to locate us. I wasn't aware of her efforts.

Then as fate would have it, a friend of my mother's was living in Miami, Florida. The friend saw a story in the Miami Herald about the Silver Knight Awards given to deserving high school students across the county. *The Miami Herald,* the sponsor of the award, ran a story in the paper about the nominees and my picture accompanied the story. My mother's friend saw the article and realized I was my mother's long-separated son. After getting that information, my mother was able to track me down. Out of the blue, I got that phone call I feared would never come.

Between the time my mother disappeared from my life until I reunited with her I learned many life lessons. But perhaps the most important one was this:

It's never too late to become what you could have been.

No matter what you have done or not done, how many mistakes you think you have made, what challenges or road blocks you've encountered in your life, there is more in you to do, be and express.

There is a dream and vision within you eagerly awaiting to manifest.

This dream does not come from outside of you, it comes from the depth of your being. It neither arises as a reaction to worldly circumstances nor does it come from marketers or commercials or from your parents. It comes from your heart. It is a call from your tomorrow.

This call is banging and knocking and calling your name. You've got to answer! When you do, you become better for it. You release more life energy and give your gifts that help evolve the society in which you live.

When you do not release that energy, there are songs that are not sung, there are books that are not written, magnificent art pieces that don't see the light of day and business ideas that go to the grave (or your urn) with you.

I couldn't understand or know this as a child, but coming home to find my mother gone was the beginning of my downward spiral to the bottom. But the situation also contained the necessary ingredients for my eventual transformation, to hijack my own life and take back my future.

And that's what I want for you...

Not the tragedy, hurt, or desperation. (Although you've probably already had your share.) But what I want for you is the experience of taking the challenges you face and transforming them into stepping-stones. Several years ago, I heard this statement: "God's gift to us is so much talent, so much energy, and so much capability we could never use it all in a single lifetime. Our gift to God is to use as much as we can during our lifetime."

The main obstacle most of us face to fulfilling our potential is not the external circumstances we face; it's not our so-called bad history or other people. The most significant obstacles are the ones we create in our minds.

Often, those self-created obstacles stem from an event that happened in our life that colors how we see ourselves. And how we see ourselves has a lot to do with how our experience will unfold; for me, I believed that my mother abandoned me. As a result of that event, I created a story that there must have been something wrong with me; I was flawed and felt less than the inherently worthy being that we all are. This belief led to a self-destructive lifestyle that nearly extinguished the possibility of me creating a life that I wanted, loved, and deserved.

Fortunately, I was able to recognize the illusion of that false identity and work through that lie and reinvent my life. If only I could go back in time and speak to that six-year-old me, I would assure him that everything was going to work out just fine. I would tell him that every challenge, every obstacle, every defeat, will help him acquire wisdom, build character, and develop strength.

But most of all, I would want to tell him that no one can hijack your future, you can take it back. I can't tell that to my six-year-old self. But I can tell it to you.

References

Allen, James, *As a Man Thinketh*. Sound Wisdom, 2019 (first published in 1903)

Ashley, Nancy, *A Seth Workbook – Create Your Own Reality*. New Awareness Network, 2014

Beckwith, Michael, *LifeVisioning*. Sounds True, 2012

Belsky, Scott, *Making Ideas Happen: Overcoming Obstacles Between Vision and Reality*. Penguin Group, 2010

Brown, Brene', *The Gifts of Imperfection: Let Go of Who Think You're Suppose to Be and Embrace Who You Are*. Hazelden Publishing, 2010

Burchard, Brendon, *High Performance Habits: How Extraordinary People Become That Way*. Hay House, 2017

Cady, H. Emilie, *Lessons In Truth*. Unity Books, 1903

Cameron, Julia, *The Artist's Way: A Spiritual Path to Higher Creativity*. Most Tacher/Putnam, 2002

Chopra, Deepak, *The Seven Spiritual Laws of Success: A Practical Guide to the Fulfillment of Your Dreams.* New World Library, 1994

Ferriss, Timothy, *The 4-Hour Workweek: Escape 9-5, Live Anywhere, and Join the New Rich.* Crown Publishers, 2009

Franklin, Imelda Octavia, *What Are You?* Martin Publishing, 2013 (First published in 1929)

Hill, Napoleon, *The Laws of Success – Original 1925 Edition.* Orne Publishing, 2020

Olsher, Steve, *What is Your What? - Discover the ONE Amazing Thing You Were Born to Do.* John Wiley and Sons, 2013

Ruiz, Don Miguel, *The Four Agreements: A Toltec Wisdom Book.* Amber-Allen Publishing, 1997

Schwartz, David J, *The Magic of Thinking Big.* Prentice-Hall Press, 195

Shinn, Florence Scovel, *The Game of Life and How to Pay It.* Devorss & Company, 1925

Sincero, Jen, *You are a Badass: How to Stop Doubting Your Greatness and Start Living An Awesome Life. Running Press, 2013*

Winfield, Chris. *"These 3 Pages Might Be Your Key to a Clearer Mind, Better Ideas, and Less Anxiety.",*

July 30, 2014. _https://www.chriswinfield.com/ morning_ *pages/*

The Holy Bible, New Revised Standard Version. World Publishing, 1997

About the Author

James Trapp is an inspirational keynote speaker, strategic advisor, and personal development coach. He brings his unique perspective to his work as a result of his experience as a trial attorney, spiritual teacher, and CEO of an international non-profit corporation. By combining universal spiritual principles with Enlightened Leadership business practices, he has helped and inspired countless people to transform their lives, achieve their goals, and elevate their organizations.

As the founder of Star Human Capital, James facilitates workshops, seminars, online courses and speaks internationally. He is the creator of The Life Liberation Method that helps people transform their mindset to achieve success in any area of their life. James is also a recipient to the Key to the City of Miami for his contributions to the community.

You can find more about James at www.jamestrapp.com.

www.ingramcontent.com/pod-product-compliance
Lightning Source LLC
Chambersburg PA
CBHW031255060726
47590CB00003B/922